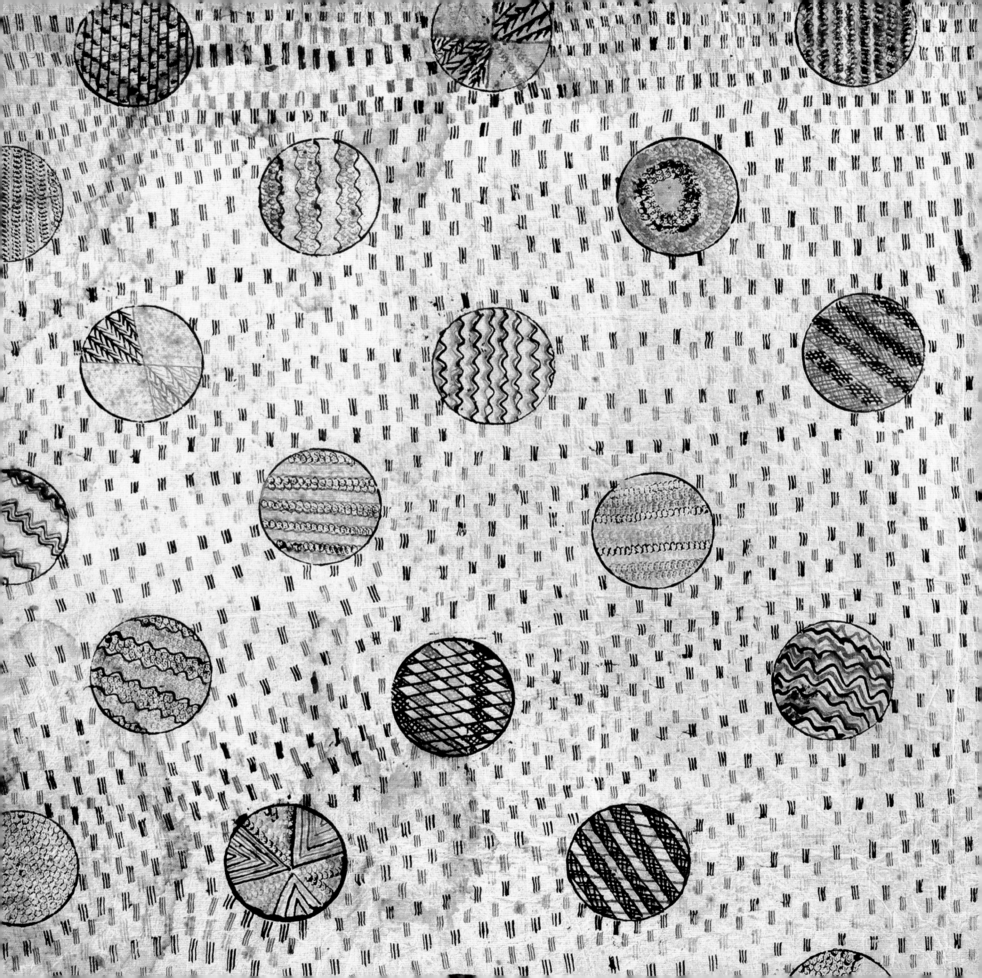

KAPUNAHOU

IN CELEBRATION OF THE

ONE HUNDRED AND SEVENTY-FIFTH ANNIVERSARY

OF THE 1841 FOUNDING OF

PUNAHOU SCHOOL

FEATURING PHOTOGRAPHS OF THE PUNAHOU CAMPUS BY LINNY MORRIS

HONOLULU

2016

Contents

opening suite of illustrations

page i

The hala tree is central to both the legend of Kapunahou and the Punahou School seal. Hawaiian scholar Mary Kawena Pukui, who taught at the school in the 1930s, noted the tree's significance for the school, "… just as the hala tree has many uses, so shall the children educated at this school be useful to Hawaii."

page ii

A kapa moe (bed covering) thought to have been given to Rev. Hiram Bingham by Queen Kaʻahumanu. An ardent convert to Christianity, the queen helped promote the missionaries' cause. In 1832, as her health declined, Kaʻahumanu asked to be transported from her Honolulu residence to her cottage in upper Mānoa. Along the way, she stopped at Kapunahou to take refreshment from its spring waters. During the queen's final days, Rev. Bingham presented her with a newly printed copy of the New Testament in Hawaiian, bound in red Moroccan leather, which she deemed "maikaʻi." Kaʻahumanu passed away at her cottage on June 5, 1832.

page iii

An 1824 drawing of chiefs Boki and Liliha by English artist John Hayter. Boki and his wife Liliha are spectacularly depicted as high-ranking chiefs. It is they who oversaw the lands of Kapunahou in the early 1800s. Liliha was given the land by her father, Hoapili, after he had inherited it from his father, Kameʻeiamoku, who had received it from Kamehameha I in 1795, following the Battle of Nuʻuanu.

pages iv–v

Rev. William Patterson Alexander, one of the founders of Punahou School, and his wife, Mary Ann McKinney, were stationed in Waiʻoli, Kauaʻi, from 1834 to 1843. On his way to Waiʻoli in the early 1840s, Alfred Agate, an artist attached to the US Exploring Expedition, encountered Alexander preaching in the kukui grove of Pīlaʻa. An eloquent preacher and noted scholar, Alexander served as a school trustee from 1853 to 1876.

pages vi

Punahou School is renowned for its hedges of night-blooming cereus that, during the summer months, bloom with flushes of large, white, clove-scented flowers. These open after sunset and last through the morning of the following day.

pages viii–ix

Alumni Reunion 2014. Kapunahou is the spiritual, historical, and cultural heart of the school. Each year more than 2,500 alumni return for Lūʻau to reaffirm their connections to the school and to one another.

page x

A 1938 Punahou School class ring featuring the Oahu College seal designed by Viggo Jacobsen in 1899. Punahou School was renamed Oahu College in 1857 to highlight the school's aim of also providing a two-year, post-secondary education; the trustees reinstated the name Punahou School in 1934. In 1940 the school adopted the current Punahou Centennial seal designed by Honolulu artist Matthew Viener, which added night-blooming cereus to the symbolic hala, spring, and kalo.

editorial note

Historians David W. Forbes '60 and Lynn Ann Davis generously provided information regarding the nineteenth-century portraits of persons associated with Punahou. In preparing the captions, we have relied significantly on material from Punahou 1841–1941, published in 1941, and Punahou: The History and Promise of a School of the Islands, published in 1991. Individuals who attended Punahou for at least a semester are considered members of the alumni body. Class year, or span of attendance for students prior to 1900, is included following the names of alumni.

This book is published by Punahou School in 2016 on the occasion of the 175th anniversary of the founding of the school in 1841.

175TH STEERING COMMITTEE MEMBERS
Ethan D. B. Abbott '72
Deborah Berger '82
Daniel H. Case '42
Wendy B. Crabb
Judith M. Sheehan '57 Dawson
Claire Olsen '58 Johnson
Duncan MacNaughton '62
Michael A. Pietsch '64
James K. Scott '70
Jeffrey N. Watanabe
Kitty Sullivan '75 Wo

STAFF
Kathryn Nelson, Vice President for Institutional Advancement; Laurel Bowers '71 Husain, Director of Communications; Kikilia Fordham '82, Director of Advancement Initiatives; Kylee Mar, Archivist; Caren Wun '86 Fukushima, Executive Assistant

Publication development and coordination by Carlyn Tani '69 in association with Barbara Pope '69 Book Design

Sam '55 and Mary Moragne '54 Cooke generously allowed the use of images from their art and library collection (pp. iii, iv–v, xvi–xvii, xviii, 63, 118)

Copyright © 2016 Punahou School, Honolulu
WWW.PUNAHOU.EDU

Library of Congress Control Number 2015951786
ISBN 978-0-692531-10-5

Designed and produced by Barbara Pope Book Design
Printed in China

Children of Rev. Peter and Fanny Gulick were among the first students attending Punahou, and the two youngest are depicted here. The only girl among seven boys, Julia Ann Eliza Gulick (1856–62) was adored by her brothers. In 1860, while a student at Punahou, she posed for this portrait. Her hair is curled in the style of the day and she wears black-lace mitts, a popular party accessory.

Her brother, Thomas Lafon Gulick (1845–60), dignified with his gold watch chain, recalled his days at Punahou, "… sliding at breakneck speed on the slippery pili grass down the steep sides of Round Top. A stone, a hillock, or a cross-trail would often toss us high in the air, but it only added to the sport." Both later worked internationally as missionaries. Fluent in Japanese, Julia retired to Hawai'i in 1909 and continued in social work among women in the Japanese community.

Dear Sir—

Samuel & Luther arrived yesterday and brought a letter from you informing that the former had been suspended from school for a term, and would be received back on making a suitable apology and promising to do better

The Millses last year spoke in high terms of Samuel's good behavior; while Henry Johnson and one or two others were said to have been well nigh expelled for bad conduct

Samuel is no doubt worthy of censure and very likely in many things. He is too easily influenced by school companions—as for instance in the case of Joe Emerson. As I understand, there has never been any misunderstanding between them and Samuel owes him no grudge, and he was foolish to allow himself to be set on by others. He was afraid of offending them

We have had a long talk with him about the "liquor" He assures

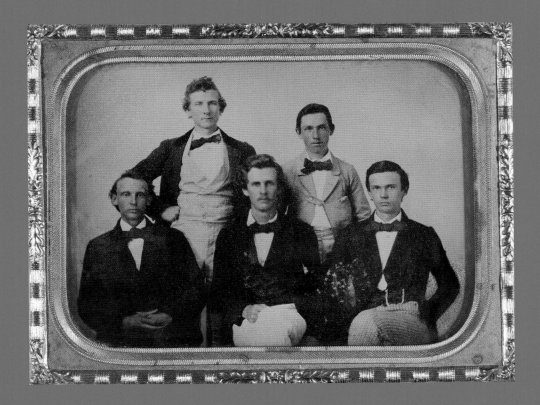

Seated: William H. Gulick (1842–60), Nathaniel B. Emerson (1849–61), and Thomas L. Gulick (1845–60). Standing: Samuel T. Alexander (1842–60) and Albert B. Lyons (1857–63).

These young men had just returned from an arduous expedition to Hawai'i Island to witness the spectacular January 1859 eruption of Mauna Loa. Each of them would lead accomplished, adventurous lives. William and Thomas Gulick served abroad as missionaries. Civil War veteran and physician Nathaniel Emerson served as president of the Hawaiian Board of Health and is known for his English translations of Hawaiian texts and his publications of traditions related to Pele.

Emerson served as a Punahou School trustee from 1882 to 1901. Samuel Alexander joined the Gold Rush of 1857 and later cofounded Alexander & Baldwin; Punahou's Alexander Field is named in his honor. Albert Lyons became the government chemist for the Kingdom of Hawaii and chaired the science department at Punahou. An outstanding teacher, Lyons inspired a love of nature among his students, including the grandson of Rev. Hiram and Sybil Bingham. Hiram Bingham III (1892) led the 1911 Yale Peruvian Expedition that brought Machu Picchu to world attention.

This panoramic oil painting of Mānoa Valley from Waikīkī in 1908, by D. Howard Hitchcock, shows the wide and deep valley that is home to Punahou School. The ahupuaʻa of Mānoa extends from the mountain summit to the sea and includes the ʻili ʻāina, or land district, of Kapunahou. The fresh water depicted in the foreground would have been near today's Ala Wai. Hilo-born artist D. Howard Hitchcock (1878–81), regarded as one of the premiere landscape artists of Hawaiʻi, taught at Punahou in 1903 and 1905–1912.

INTRODUCTION

JAMES K. SCOTT '70

Ka'ahumanu, descended from chiefs that ruled over Maui and Hawai'i Island, rose to prominence as the favorite wife of Kamehameha I. According to historian Samuel M. Kamakau, Hawaiians said that "Of Kamehameha's two possessions, his wife and his kingdom," Ka'ahumanu "was the more beautiful."

Louis Choris, the French artist who accompanied the 1815–18 worldwide expedition led by Russian explorer Otto von Kotzebue, made the watercolor sketch of Ka'ahumanu on which this lithograph was based. She is shown at Kamehameha's Kailua-Kona court in 1817, wrapped in kapa with a feather lei on her head and a small kahili in her hand, symbols of her chiefly rank.

After Kamehameha's death in 1819, Ka'ahumanu served as kuhina nui, or regent, alongside Liholiho (Kamehameha II). When the missionaries arrived in 1820, they found that Ka'ahumanu and the young Liholiho had overthrown the traditional religion of Hawai'i. Bereft of the structure provided by traditional rituals and gods, Hawaiian society was in transition and receptive to the Christian missionaries and their teachings. In 1829, Ka'ahumanu prevailed upon her cousins, the chiefs Boki and Liliha, to give the lands of Kapunahou to Rev. Hiram Bingham.

Punahou School has risen from its humble origins as an adobe-and-thatch schoolhouse, founded in May 1841, to become the largest single-campus independent K–12 school in America. On the 175th anniversary of that founding, we celebrate this extraordinary institution. The school's longevity and size, together with stability and continuity in leadership, have forged a modern institution that is a global leader in educational innovation.

I have been honored to serve as president of Punahou since 1994, building upon the leadership of Rod McPhee and others before him who advanced the school's reputation for academic excellence. Early in my tenure, I came to appreciate that the school's singular mission and vision stem from two historic gifts that set the foundation for today: the gift of land from Hawaiian ali'i and the gift of an educational vision from Protestant missionaries. Our New England heritage of scholarly achievement, coupled with our Hawaiian reverence for place, inspires a philosophy of educational renewal that thrives within a campus of timeless beauty.

Ancient Hawaiians prized the land of Kapunahou, nestled in the fertile ahupua'a of Mānoa, for the life-giving freshwater spring at its core. In 1795, King Kamehameha I awarded Kapunahou to his loyal chief Kame'eiamoku after the triumphant Battle of Nu'uanu. Kame'eiamoku later entrusted the lands to his son, Hoapili, who for twenty years resided in the vicinity of the spring. Kamehameha I was a frequent guest at Hoapili's home and often walked the surrounding grounds.

From the time of Kamehameha I, control of all land in Hawai'i remained in the hands of the ruling chief; however, land inheritance for high-ranking chiefs like Hoapili was allowed. Hoapili in time gave Kapunahou to his daughter, Liliha, and her husband, Boki. In 1829, at the urging of ruling chief Queen Ka'ahumanu, an avid supporter of Christianity, the couple granted custody of Kapunahou to the Reverend Hiram Bingham, leader of the missionary community in Hawai'i. Liliha initially resisted the conveyance of land, but Boki proceeded with entrusting its custody to Bingham before departing on an expedition to the South Pacific. Ka'ahumanu served as konohiki, or landlord, for Kapunahou. She had a thatched house erected for herself near the spring and an adobe-and-thatch cottage for the Binghams near the present Old School Hall. Boki was lost in a disaster at sea and never returned, and Kapunahou remained under Bingham's, and thus the Sandwich Islands Mission's, stewardship.

After the Mahele of 1848 instituted private land ownership, the American Board of Commissioners for Foreign Missions (ABCFM) sought written title to Kapunahou. John Papa 'Ī'ī, a respected adviser to Kauikeaouli (Kamehameha III) and a member of the Land Commission, was among those who testified in favor of the mission, and in 1849 the Land Commission granted the title for Kapunahou to the ABCFM.

The Protestant missionaries, who first arrived in Hawai'i in 1820, believed that education was a cornerstone of life. They devoted themselves to pioneering efforts that encompassed developing the Hawaiian alphabet, printing the first Hawaiian-language Bible and newspaper, and establishing schools for Hawaiian children on Maui, Hawai'i, and O'ahu. The demanding work left missionary parents with little time for their own children's instruction. Many of them reluctantly decided to send their boys and girls back to New England for school, causing wrenching family separations.

The missionaries' original plans for Kapunahou called for a school to serve the children of Hawaiian ali'i, but after the Chiefs' Children's School opened in Honolulu in 1839, they were able to focus on the issue of their own children's education in Hawai'i. On July 11, 1842, fifteen students from mission families took their seats in a schoolroom built amid the sugarcane fields bordering the former Bingham cottage. Punahou's first principal, the Reverend Daniel Dole, set forth the school's lofty educational goals. "We wish to have [our students] fitted to enter college at this school," he wrote in a letter to the mission. "Should any of them wish to become teachers, merchants, mechanics, or farmers, we wish to give them in this school an education which will prepare them to be respectable and highly useful in their several professions."

Today Punahou educates 3,750 students from a broad cross-section of Hawai'i, all of whom experience the school's dual legacy. Mālama 'āina, caring for the Earth, affirms our appreciation for the original gift of land. As modern stewards of a wahi pana, land that is steeped in history, we have a responsibility to cultivate the natural and cultural resources of Kapunahou. The school's focus on a revitalized campus centered on Kapunahou, combined with a renewed emphasis on Hawaiian culture and language, sustains our connection to Punahou's Hawaiian origins.

Punahou's mission calls us to cultivate the hearts, minds, and spirits of our students. The school exemplifies a student-centered learning environment, in which open inquiry, ethical action, and the lively exchange of ideas nurture each child's highest potential, drawing on our heritage of scholarly achievement. To prepare our students for their futures, we are embarking on an exciting renewal of learning environments that considers our K–12 campus as a single system, anchored by its expansive green spaces and the waters of Kapunahou. Guided by insights gained from the latest pedagogy and from the neuroscience of learning, we are about to complete

Kauikeaouli (Kamehameha III) reigned from 1825 to 1854. Under his rule, the Kingdom of Hawaii enacted its first constitution, created a legislative government, and established the Board of Commissioners to Quiet Land Titles, all of which set the stage for private ownership of land. In 1849, the Commission granted Kapunahou's title to ABCFM, the governing body of the Sandwich Islands Mission, and the government issued the school's first charter. The establishment of Oahu College in 1857 convinced ABCFM that its work in the islands was done, and the Board conveyed the lands of Kapunahou to the school.

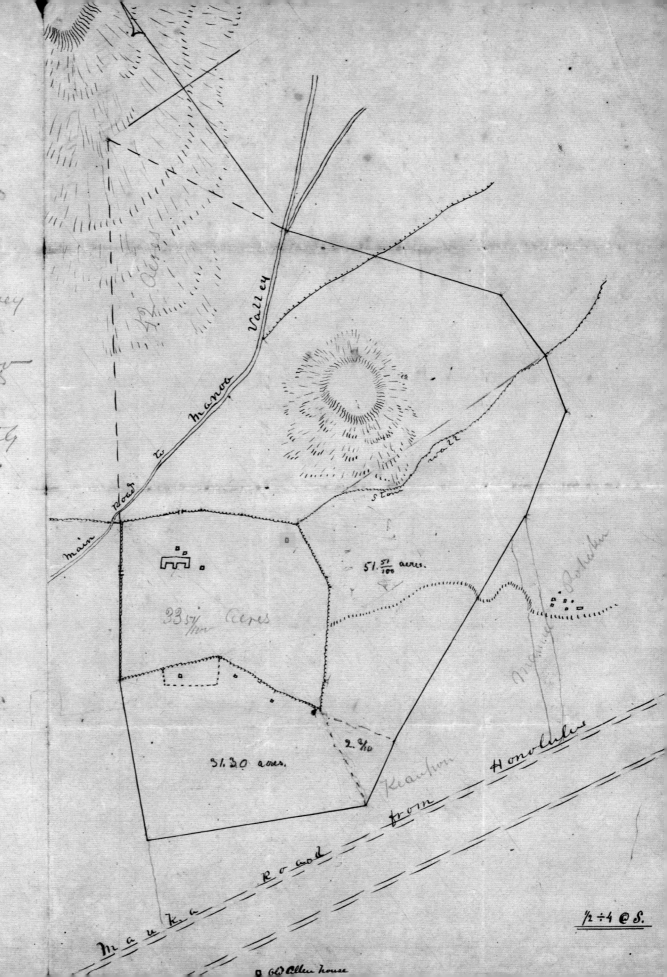

"I, Kaauwai sworn—I know this land I heard Boki say to Hoapili Kane concerning the gift of this land to the Sandwich Islands Mission that he had given it to Mr. Bingham. Boki's wife [Liliha] made some objection to giving it to Mr. Bingham claiming it as hers as received from her father Hoapili Kane, but Hoapili Kane confirmed the gift and it was adjudged to be right and proper. From what I heard at the time of the boundaries, I should think Mr. Metcalf's survey correct." March 23, 1849, testimony by Zorobabela Ka'auwai.

Ka'auwai was a member of the Land Commission, the vehicle to convert Hawaiian communal interests in land to a Western system of ownership, allowing land held in fee to be bought and sold.

Survey map of Kapunahou, 1848. This map, drawn by T. Metcalf for the American Board of Commissioners for Foreign Missions, is the first official survey of Kapunahou. The document delineates the 224.65 acres given to the mission, 76 acres of which constitute the campus today. The property originally extended from the slopes of 'Ualaka'a (Round Top) to the present grounds of Central Union Church, and included Kukuluae'o, a separate 77-acre property and related sea fishery near the current Kewalo Basin. This coveted property was separated from Kapunahou when the government clarified land claims in 1853.

The map delineates a small kuleana of 1.3 acres located on the makai side of the E-shaped building (the initial school structure) and Ka'ahumanu wall. This parcel belonged to Kauhi and his wife, Martha Pohopu, who recounted the legend of the spring to W. D. Alexander. On his homestead, Kauhi tended to lo'i kalo fed by waters from the spring (highlighted in green). In 1866, his heir, Ikeole, sold the property to Oahu College, completing the school's title to lands within the boundaries of Kapunahou.

The founding of Punahou School would not have been possible without the largesse and support of the monarchy. John Papa ʻĪʻī, a respected advisor to Kamehameha III, was a member of the Land Commission. He testified in support of the mission, "This land was given to Mr. Bingham for the Sandwich Islands Mission by Governor Boki in 1829.... I was witness to the gift. The title of the Mission is perfectly clear."

John Papa ʻĪʻī, known for his stern demeanor, adjudicated Punahou's annual examinations in 1856. Both he and Governor Mataio Kekūanāoʻa, also present, delighted in young Henry Parker's (1842–1860) winning oratory on wine, delivered in Hawaiian.

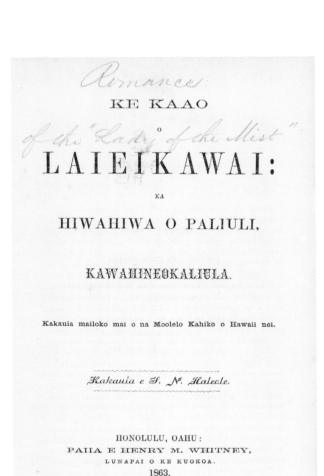

an ambitious redesign of our Junior School. Core to that redesign is a new team of leaders. In the 2015–2016 school year, Emily McCarren, former director of Wo International Center, succeeded Kevin Conway as Academy principal, while former dean Paris Priore-Kim '76, EdD succeeded Mike Walker as Junior School principal. Together, McCarren and Priore-Kim bring fresh perspectives to cultivating a student-centered environment.

Because curiosity propels learning, we envision students collaborating in flexibly configured spaces that support activities inspired by their own inquiry with guidance from their teachers. Because outdoor exploration ignites learning, we will emphasize our storied place, Kapunahou, to maximize meaningful learning within our island environment. And, because we recognize that children learn authentically through action, we plan to have our students developing projects, products, and ideas throughout a dynamic learning commons invigorated by creative makerspaces across campus.

Although Punahou is one of the most ethnically diverse schools in the 1,800-member National Association of Independent Schools, we continue to strive to be more socioeconomically diverse by welcoming talented students regardless of their family's financial circumstances. When students and faculty actively engage within a richly diverse intellectual and social environment, they learn to work together to generate ethical, transformative change not only in their own lives, but in their communities, and, often, in the world.

In 1971, Punahou welcomed a keenly observant ten-year-old who had just returned to Honolulu from living in Indonesia. He would later recall the discomfort he felt those first days at Punahou, being "a kid with a funny name in a new school, feeling a little out of place." His fifth-grade teacher, Mabel Hefty, who had just returned from a sabbatical in Kenya, took the young pupil under her wing. From her, he learned an invaluable lesson. "Ms. Hefty taught me that I had something to say," President Barack Obama later wrote, "not in spite of my differences, but because of them."

The essays in this celebratory volume explore leadership, public purpose, access and diversity, global learning, and educational innovation at Punahou, and, together, they offer a vivid portrait of a school reaching toward its highest aspirations. Kapunahou symbolizes renewal—Punahou School's ability to embrace dynamic change and forge a singular future is inspired by the founding gifts.

right

The first structure built specifically for the school in 1841 was an adobe building in the shape of an "E," combining classroom and living accommodations for teachers and student boarders. The E-Building was described as "purely a native product"— the wood for its timbers and rafters was from Mānoa Valley, the pili grass for its thatched roof was from Rocky Hill, and the plaster and whitewash were from the Kewalo reefs. Rev. Daniel Dole, principal, served as architect and builder. The two-story Rice Hall was completed in 1846 under the supervision of teacher and agriculturalist William Harrison Rice. This etching was made by Honolulu artist H. N. Poole in 1916 from an 1846 drawing by Horton O. Knapp.

In a diary entry dated July 11, 1842, Levi Chamberlain, a founding trustee of Punahou School, notes the first day of class. He describes driving his horse-drawn wagon through "some rain and a pretty strong wind" to transport his four children and two other students to and from school and the mission complex near Kawaiaha'o Church. In a wry observation that today's parents can appreciate, he wrote: "Thus begins the business of carrying and returning the children, which must be continued from day to day so long as the children remain with us and the school is conducted." Tuition was $12 a semester, with three semesters constituting the school year.

Old School Hall, completed in December 1851, is the oldest building on campus. The two-story structure was laid upon a foundation of coral slabs and built with stone quarried from Rocky Hill. Student Samuel T. Alexander (1860) described the layout: "The upper story is used for the school room and the lower for recitation room, library room, and a splendid cabinet [to display shells, minerals and fossils]."

Near Old School Hall, a stone tablet and brass plaque mark the site of Hiram and Sybil Bingham's adobe cottage, built in 1831. It was here that Rev. Bingham worked on translating the Bible into Hawaiian. Sybil Bingham recalled her own labors, "Beginning at the lanai of the house we went onward, with some hoomanawanui [fortitude] indeed, till old walls were leveled and taro beds and deep pits, from which [adobe] bricks had been made, were raised and the smooth rich surface of the whole stocked with cane and its entire border planted with bananas." The Bingham's first cottage at Punahou was a grass house provided in 1830 by Ka'ahumanu.

overleaf

In February 1839, Edwin O. Hall, missionary printer wrote "...I have a great hope that the year 1839 will see this nation in possession of the whole bible in their own language. But one edition of 10,000 copies will not begin to go round and give all that want it a copy."

In 1839, Hall completed the printing and binding of the first complete edition of the Bible in Hawaiian. At nearly a thousand pages, the book quickly became known as "ka buke poepoe" (the rotund or fat book). It was the culmination of nearly twenty years of translation performed by a team of missionaries that included Revs. Lorrin Andrews, Hiram Bingham, Artemas Bishop, Ephraim Clark, Sheldon Dibble, Jonathan Green, William Richards, and Asa Thurston.

The 1843 leather-bound edition of Ka Palapala Hemolele (The Holy Bible) featured on the following page is part of the significant collection of nineteenth-century Hawaiian-language imprints in the Punahou School Archives. Kenneth Emory (1916), famed Pacific anthropologist, recalled spending hours in Cooke Library, "in that little room they had, the Gorham Gilman Room, ...I would take advantage of his books on Hawai'i and the South Seas." Kenneth was the son of Walter Emory, one of the architects for Castle Hall.

Ka Palapala Hemolele a Iehova ko Kakou Akua, O Ke Kauoha Kahiko a me O Ke Kauoha Hou *(The Holy Scriptures of Jehova Our God, The Old Testament and The New Testament) 1843, with the original full-leather binding. Pages from the Book of Joshua (Iosua) and the Book of Judges (Lunakanawai) are depicted here.*

IOSUA.

na kanaka, He poe hoike oukou no oukou iho, ua koho oukou ia Iehova no oukou, e malama aku ia ia. Olelo aku la lakou, He poe hoike no makou.

23 Ano la, e kipaku oukou i na'kua e, mai ko oukou alo aku, a e hoopili oukou me ko oukou naau ia Iehova i ke Akua o ka Iseraela.

24 Olelo aku la na kanaka ia Iosua, O Iehova, o ko kakou Akua, o ka makou ia e malama aku ai a o kona leo ka makou e hoolohe aku ai.

25 A hana iho la o Iosua i berita me na kanaka i kela la, a waiho oia no lakou i ke kanawai a me ke kapu ma Sekema.

26 A kakau iho la o Iosua i keia mau olelo maloko o ka buke o ke kanawai o ke Akua, a lawe no hoi oia i pohaku nui a kukulu iho la i ua pohaku la malaila, ma ka laau e kokoke ana i ka halelewa o Iehova.

27 Olelo aku la o Iosua i na kanaka a pau, Eia hoi keia pohaku, oia ko kakou mea hoike, no ka mea, ua lohe ia mea i na olelo a pau a Iehova, ana i kauoha mai ai ia kakou, a he mea hoike no ia no oukou o hoole oukou i ke Akua.
476

28 A hookuu aku la o Iosua i ka poe kanaka, i kela kanaka i keia kanaka i kona aina.

29 Mahope iho o keia mau mea, make iho la o Iosua, ke keiki a Nuna, ke kauwa a Iehova, a o kona mau la a pau, hookahi ia haneri makahiki a me ka umi keu.

30 A kanu iho la lakou ia ia ma ke kihi o kona aina, ma Timenasera, ma ka puu o Eperaima, ma ke kukulu akau o ka puu o Gaasa.

31 A malama no ka Iseraela ia Iehova i na la a pau o Iosua, a i na la a pau o na lunakahiko, i ola mahope iho o Iosua, ka poe i ike i na mea a pau a Iehova i hana mai ai i ka Iseraela.

32 A o na iwi o Iosepa a na mamo a Iseraela i lawe mai ai, mai Aigupita mai, kanu iho la lakou ia mea ma Sekema, i kahi ma ke kula a Iakoba i kuai ai me na keiki a Hemora, ka makua o Sekema, i na moni hookahi haneri, a ili mai ho ia na na keiki a Iosepa.

33 A make o Eleazara ke keiki a Aarona, a kanu iho la lakou ia ia ma ka puu o Pinehasa o kana keiki, i haawiia mai nona ma ka puu o Eperaima.

LUNAKANAWAI.

MOKUNA I.

Ke kaua ana o ka Iseraela i ko Kanaana, a pio ko Kanaana, a me ka Pereza, a me ko Ierusalema, a me ko Heberona, aole nae i pau na kanaka i ka make.

MAHOPE iho o ka make ana o Iosua, ninau aku la ka poe mamo a Iseraela ia Iehova, i aku la, Owai ko makou mea e pii mua aku i ke alo o ko Kanaana, e kaua aku ia lakou?

2 I mai la o Iehova, E pii ae ka Iuda, aia hoi, ua haawi au i ka aina i kona lima.

3 I ae la, ka Iuda i ka Simeona, i kona kaikuaana, E hele pu oe me au, ma ko'u kuleana, i kaua aku kakou i ko Kanaana, a e hele pu no hoi au me oe, ma kou hele ana. A hele pu aku la ka Simeona me ia.

4 Pii aku la ka Iuda, a haawi mai la o Iehova i ko Kanaana, a me ka Pereza, i ko lakou lima. A luku aku la lakou i kela poe ma Bezeka, he umi tausani kanaka.

5 A ma Bezeka, loaa ia lakou o Adonibezeka, a kaua aku la lakou ia ia, a luku aku la lakou i ko Kanaana, a me ka Pereza.

6 Holo aku la o Adonibezeka, a hahai aku la lakou ia ia, a loaa oia, alaila ooki ae la lakou i na manamana nui, o kona mau lima, a me na manamana nui o kona mau wawae.

7 I ae la o Adonibezeka, He kanahiku alii, ua okiia na manamana nui o ko lakou lima, a me ko lakou wawae, hoiliili lakou malalo iho o ko'u papaaina. E like me ka'u i hana aku ai, pela i hoopai mai ai ke Akua ia'u. Lawe ae la lakou ia ia i Ierusalema, a malaila ia i make ai.

8 ¶ Ua kaua aku ka poe mamo a Iuda, a ua hoopio, a ua luku aku ia Ierusalema, i ka maka o ka pahikaua, a ua puhi aku ia kulanakauhale i ke ahi.

9 A mahope iho hele ae la na mamo a Iuda e kaua aku i ko Kanaana, i ka poe i noho ma ka mauna, a ma ka aoao hema, a ma ka papu.

10 Hele ku e aku la ka Iuda i ko Kanaana, i ka poe i noho ma Heberona; (o Kiriatareba ka inoa kahiko o Heberona) a pepehi aku la lakou ia Sesai, a me Ahimana, a me Talemai.

11 A malaila aku lakou i hele ai e ku e i Debira; (o Kiritesepera ka inoa kahiko o Debira.)

12 I iho la o Kaleba, O ka
477

opposite

Sybil Bingham planted the first slips of night-blooming cereus near the front entrance of Kapunahou in 1836. This striking nocturnal plant, known as pānini o kapunahou, now covers the outer stone walls of the school and adorns the school seal. The cactus is said to have arrived in Hawai'i in 1831 aboard a trading vessel returning from Mazatlan, Mexico.

Dedicated in 1934, the front gates of the school open to Chamberlain Field and Palm Drive, lined with palms first planted in 1894. Students in Punahou's J. B. Castle School of Manual Arts designed and constructed the gates under the supervision of John Mahony, teacher, and Hart Wood, one of a select group of early twentieth-century architects affiliated with a distinctive island style of architecture.

In 1831, Ka'ahumanu urged her brother, Kuakini, the governor of O'ahu, to build a stone wall along the lower edge of Kapunahou to protect its uplands from cattle. To mark the land's makai boundary, Kauikeaouli (Kamehameha III) ordered that an immense stone called Pōhakuloa be moved from the slopes of 'Ualaka'a (Round Top). In the 1850s, Pōhakuloa was broken into pieces to make way for the widening of Punahou Street. Historians Elspeth Petrie '35 Sterling and Catherine Cooke '36 Summers say that the single upright stone that stands at the right of Punahou's main entrance may be a remnant from this sacred stone.

Chief Abner Pākī was the father of Bernice Pauahi Bishop and the hānai father of Lili'uokalani. Historians Laura Green and Mary Kawena Pukui recount that after men dug out the enormous stone Pōhakuloa, the question arose as to who should lift it. "Chief Paki was a very powerful man, said to have been seven feet in height. He took hold of the stone and lifted it upright."

13

Montague Hall, named in honor of Juliette Montague Cooke and her daughter, Juliette Montague Cooke (1850–63) Atherton, opened in 1937 as a state-of-the-art facility dedicated to the instruction of music. Montague Hall is home to the school's orchestras and the Punahou Music School, which serves 950 students each year, including pupils from the broader community.

Designed by architects Charles W. Dickey and Roy C. Kelley, Montague Hall was made possible through a gift from the Juliette M. Atherton Trust and members of the Atherton family. Dickey's use of Spanish Colonial and Mediterranean proportions and motifs is tempered by his architectural references to the dominant roof of Hawaiian thatched houses and the simplicity and plastered adobe of the early missionary buildings in the islands.

opposite
Montague Hall, with its accent of musical notes overlooking the entry court, reflects the distinctive style that emerged in Charles W. Dickey's work in the late 1920s in Hawai'i. In both his commercial and residential work, Dickey favored recessed spaces, cream-colored stucco walls, a graceful sloping roof, and green and russet variegated tiles. In addition to Montague Hall, Dickey designed Punahou's Alexander Hall and Wilcox Hall, all built in the 1930s.

His trademark "Dickey roof," a double-pitched hipped roof often featuring expansive eaves and Asian-derived detailing, has become part of Hawai'i's building vernacular. Examples of Dickey's work in Honolulu today include the Harkness Building at The Queen's Medical Center, the US Immigration Office, and the Alexander & Baldwin Building.

Hugo Stangenwald photographed Amos Starr Cooke and his wife, Juliette Montague Cooke, with two of their seven children in 1853. The Cookes headed the Chiefs' Children's School, a boarding school in Honolulu primarily for the children of ali'i. Their students included Princess Bernice Pauahi and five future monarchs, including Lydia Kamaka'eha (Lili'uokalani).

After leaving the school and the mission, Amos Cooke joined Samuel N. Castle in founding Castle & Cooke, Inc. He is shown here with daughter Mary Annis (1859–64), who later became a concert vocalist performing under the name Annis Montague.

Juliette Montague Cooke believed in the power of music, calling it "an expression of the emotions of the heart." She had a beautiful voice, and wove music into the curriculum of the Chiefs' Children's School. She is shown here with son Amos Francis. Daughter Juliette Montague Cooke (1850–63) Atherton became a lifelong advocate for education and culture in Hawai'i. Montague Hall honors the contributions of these two accomplished women and their families.

opposite

Pauahi Hall was built in 1896 as a tribute to the late Bernice Pauahi by her husband, Charles Reed Bishop. The new structure held classrooms, administrative offices, and the library, auditorium, and art gallery. For nearly forty years, the life of the school centered around Pauahi Hall, and for generations, students and alumni have gathered for class photographs on its front steps.

This Victorian-era building, constructed from gray basalt quarried from nearby Judd Hillside, was designed by architects Arthur Reynolds and Clinton Ripley. Charles W. Dickey served as the project's architectural supervisor. Ripley and Dickey designed Hawaiian Hall at Bernice Pauahi Bishop Museum, built in 1903.

Bernice Pauahi Bishop, descendant of Kamehameha I, was the daughter of Abner Pākī and Laura Konia. She attended the Chiefs' Children's School, where she was a star pupil of the Cookes. In 1850, she married American businessman and banker Charles Reed Bishop; they are shown here c. 1859. Following Pauahi's death in 1884, her will established the Kamehameha Schools in 1887. Charles served as a Punahou trustee from 1867 to 1891 and was a major school benefactor. Charles's gifts supported the school's endowment, scholarships for Hawaiian students, and the construction of Bishop Hall of Science (1884; removed in 1959), Charles R. Bishop Hall (1901; rebuilt in 1972) and Pauahi Hall.

Cooke Hall, which opened as a library in 1909, was built from dark basalt likely quarried near the school grounds. The building is named for Charles Montague Cooke (1861–66) and his wife, Anna Charlotte Rice (1867–68) Cooke.

Charles, son of Amos and Juliette Cooke, served as a school trustee from 1880 to 1898. Anna, daughter of missionaries William Harrison and Mary Hyde Rice, was born at Punahou School in 1853 and is best remembered as the founder of the Honolulu Academy of Arts, today's Honolulu Museum of Art.

Cooke Hall was designed by Harry Livingston Kerr, a prominent Honolulu architect of the 1920s–30s. He also designed the original McKinley High School (today's Linekona School, Honolulu Museum of Art), Maui County Courthouse, and Kaumakapili Church.

After the construction of the current Cooke Library in 1965, also funded by the Cooke family endowment, Cooke Hall underwent renovations and today houses administrative and faculty offices along with classrooms.

Emma Metcalf (Nakuina)

Emma Metcalf (1852–1865) Beckley Nakuina was one of the school's first Hawaiian students. She enrolled a decade after Punahou first opened its doors, and later attended Mills Seminary in California. As a member of the court of Alexander Liholiho (Kamehameha IV), Nakuina was a respected authority on Hawaiian culture and served as a judge and a commissioner on water rights. She was also the first curator for the Hawaiian National Museum, which later formed the early collections of Bishop Museum.

In Honolulu in the 1850s it was possible to have portraits taken by new photographic processes, the daguerreotype and the ambrotype. Many of the photographs of persons associated with Punahou's early years are the work of Hugo Stangenwald, one of the most successful photographers working in the islands between 1853 and 1858.

The fragile images, printed on a polished surface, required protection and were often placed in hinged cases that fit into one's hand and opened like a small book. Nā pa'i ki'i—delicately tinted photographic images rich with detail—eased the pain of separation from family members in New England, including children who went away for schooling. "Pa'i" means to print, as in printing kapa; "ki'i" is the word for image.

Kaakau, photographed in a patterned holokū with a hibiscus in her hair, lived at Kualoa with the Wilder family. Elizabeth Kina'u Judd (1842–45) Wilder, one of the first students at Punahou, was the eldest daughter of missionaries Gerrit P. Judd, physician, and Laura Fish Judd. Elizabeth's husband, Samuel G. Wilder, became a partner with Dr. Judd in a sugar plantation at Kualoa in 1864, and the Wilders resided there with their children: Willie, Laura (1875–76), Gerrit (1877–81), and Samuel Jr. (1879–81), who was born in a grass house at Kualoa in 1866.

Kaakau was young Gerrit's nurse. In her memoirs, Elizabeth recalled the sad occasion of Kaakau's death at Kualoa in 1867 (a few years after this portrait was taken) and the wailing of Hawaiian women around her coffin on the veranda.

The plantation proved a failure, and in 1867 the Wilders relocated to Judd Street in Honolulu. Elizabeth recalled, "The next summer we returned for the children's vacation, while the mill was grinding its last crop. Willie was absolutely happy to be at Kualoa again, visiting all the familiar spots, capering and whistling with delight. He was a dear little boy, right and affectionate, beloved by all for his sweet nature." That summer, Willie, then nine years old, died from injuries suffered in an accident at the mill.

William Chauncey Wilder's portrait (right) was made at Kualoa sometime between 1864 and 1868. The fishpond and a row of houses, possibly thatched, can be seen in the background. Wilder Avenue on the makai border of Punahou School is named for his father, Samuel G. Wilder, prominent in shipping and government.

This portrait captures the proud, no-nonsense demeanor of Poakahi, a member of the bustling Chamberlain household, which included Levi, Maria, and their eight children. After Levi Chamberlain's death in 1849, Maria supported herself and the household by taking in boarders.

Shortly after arriving safely in Boston in 1850 after a challenging voyage around Cape Horn, the two oldest Chamberlain daughters, Maria Jane (1842–50) and Martha Ann (1842–50), had their portraits taken to send back home. In a letter to the girls, attending Mount Holyoke Seminary, their mother, Maria Chamberlain, described the response from Poakahi and other family members when the package was unwrapped.

"The children had just returned from school [Punahou]. As we had been anticipating their [the daguerreotypes] arrival with great interest, I thought I would not exhibit them till after tea and worship. But Isabella [1844–58] found a wrapper, and on it [was] marked Daguerreotypes. She was wild with excitement. She jumped and laughed, and pulled my arm to go for them, but I said come to supper first— she could not eat any.

After worship we gathered round the table and old Poakahi coming in to express her opinion amongst the rest—Mr. G. [Goodale] thought you looked cold. The boys said you were made far too black, their sisters were fair. Isabella said they did not look half so well as her sisters. Poakahi said, it is them, but they should have taken off their kiheis [shawls]— that makes them look like old women. . . . I know my dear Maria Jane that you had a great desire that those pictures should give us pleasure, but you must not think much of it."

This ambrotype portrait of Maria Chamberlain made in the 1860s was considered a good likeness and conveyed her sense of propriety. Both her husband, Levi Chamberlain, and her grandson, William W. Chamberlain (1882–92), served as Punahou School trustees. Chamberlain Field and Chamberlain Drive are named for William, who served from 1914 to 1937.

LEADERSHIP

JAMES KOSHIBA '91

Knowing his calendar would fill quickly, I had booked a series of interviews with President Jim Scott '70 well in advance. I'd also asked if we could spend one appointment walking around campus instead of talking in his office. I was surprised when he jumped at the request. "I prefer that we walk, actually." On a clear fall afternoon we depart the President's Office. Barely outside the Sullivan Administration Building, Jim makes the first of many stops. "Excuse me for just a minute." About twenty members of the custodial staff are assembled in front of Dillingham Hall, reporting for the evening shift. I hang back and watch as they exchange smiles and banter with Jim. He rejoins me a minute later. "The crew gathers here every day around this time," he says, as we walk on.

Every few yards, we stop for a chat with a member of the faculty or staff. We cross the Academy grounds and students greet him sporadically, "Howzit, Dr. Scott?" Some pause long enough for a passing handshake or a nod of acknowledgement. No one is surprised to see the president roaming. Formalities are neither expected nor offered, and no student drops what he or she is doing. "Students get out on the half hour, so that's when I try to get around."

Once we leave behind the crowds of the Academy, we stop at the campus's landmarks. Each site holds some personal significance for Jim. At the Mamiya Science Center, he says, "This was the first building project after I became president." At the steps of the cafeteria, he notes, "When I was a student, all the kids on financial aid worked on-campus jobs. I washed dishes." At each spot, there's a story. Storytelling comes naturally to Jim—his colleagues see it as one of his gifts.

We spend an hour this way, circling the campus and stopping for stories. Nearly back to the Sullivan Building, we make a final stop at the Wo International Center. "When I came to campus to interview for the job of president, I saw the Wo Center [then newly constructed], and I thought, 'That's where we used to slide down the hill!' It was impressive, but there was a sense of loss, too."

In the world of independent schools, it's rare for an individual to become head of the school from which he or she graduated. Jim sees his alumnus status as a crucial asset. "I can relate to alumni and long-time faculty," he says. "People know I'm pushing change, but they also feel confident that I'm not going to abandon the history of the place."

Schools are notoriously difficult places to change. More than any institution, they are steeped in tradition and collective memory—from proms and frog dissections to *Lord of the Flies* and homecoming week. Some of Punahou's traditions span a century or more, with distinctive

rituals like Third Grade Lūʻau, Camp Timberline, and the Punahou Carnival, in addition to the usual customs of American schooling.

Shared memories build community—our attachment to them is our attachment to each other. As a result of this attachment, it's hard for schools to let anything go. Taking frog dissections out of the science curriculum, or Shakespeare off the reading list, can prompt pitched political battles, as many a school reformer can attest.

One might expect that a school with 175 years of history would find change more difficult than most. Yet Punahou has managed a series of transformations. Some are obvious—more than $120 million in capital projects, including the Mamiya Science Center, Luke Center for Public Service, Case Middle School, and Omidyar K–1 Neighborhood. Other changes are less visible but no less dramatic: Punahou's endowment has nearly tripled, and enrollment remained strong through the worst economy since the Great Depression.

The media footprint of the school has expanded enormously. Since the start of the new millennium, Punahou has been named the greenest school in America; *Sports Illustrated* twice ranked its athletics program the best in the nation; it graduated a high-profile Heisman Trophy candidate (Manti Teʻo '09), an LPGA tournament champion (Michelle Wie '07), and a world-champion surfer (Carissa Moore '10); and US President Barack Obama graduated from Punahou in 1979.

Most important, teaching and learning at Punahou have changed. Entrepreneurship, sustainability, global citizenship, public service, project-based learning—these pillars of instruction today occupied little curricular real estate twenty years ago. The science of brain development and the neurology of learning now shape classroom and curricular design. Laptops are ubiquitous, edible gardens flourish in previously unused corners of campus, and students work in the community in ways few people would have imagined two decades ago. Standing at the epicenter of these changes, and instigating many of them, has been Jim Scott.

Jim is a natural storyteller, but he started his tenure with intentional quiet. In his opening address to the faculty in 1994—just after Punahou hired him as president—Jim pledged to spend an entire year asking and listening before unveiling any new plans. He made good on his promise, engaging faculty, students, staff, alumni, parents, trustees, and community partners in conversation—paying close attention, posing tough questions, and probing for ideas wherever he could. He explored Punahou's history, combing the archives for stories of the school's beginnings, its leaders, and its prominent personalities. He reflected upon the school's past and his own experience as a student.

The next fall, Jim shared his aspirations for Punahou—seven vision statements encompassing instruction, character education, financial aid, school management, and Punahou's role in the community. Over the next two decades, these concepts would give rise to some of Punahou's defining initiatives, including commitments to global education, service, sustainability, access, and socioeconomic diversity.

While he pressed the Punahou community to embrace a new vision, Jim also began to tell new stories about the school. Some of the stories he told were new takes on old narratives. He gave the legend of Kapunahou fresh significance by highlighting the cultural importance of water to the Hawaiian people. "Water was so precious, it was life," he said. "The Hawaiian word for water is *wai*, and the word for wealth is *waiwai*. Land with a flowing spring was a treasure."

Jim shared stories of his own heroes and mentors: His seventh-grade science teacher, Dave Eldredge '49, was the first teacher to ask him about college plans, walking Jim to Cooke Library and instructing him to read the catalog for Stanford University (where Jim would earn his undergraduate degree a decade later). Al Harrington '54 had him set goals—athletic and academic—that would prepare him to excel later in life.

Like his predecessors, he paid tribute to the work of the Protestant missionaries who founded Punahou School so they would no longer have to endure the heartbreak of sending their children "back East" for an education. To this familiar founding tale he added a new story: the gift of the land, Kapunahou, from Ka'ahumanu, the favorite wife of Kamehameha I and coregent with Liholiho (Kamehameha II) and Kauikeaouli (Kamehameha III).

Telling the two stories together was intentional. "I talk about the two gifts," Jim explains, "the gift of the school built by the missionaries, and the gift of land from the monarchy. There's a Hawaiian root to go along with the Christian root. There's a tension in that, but also a calling."

The stories worked hand in hand with his vision. The phrases he used are now well known to anyone who graduated during his tenure. "To whom much is given, much is expected" was a sentiment then–Senator-elect Barack Obama reinforced when he spoke to students at Punahou in 2004. "Private school with a public purpose" was a guiding principle in many faculty discussions. These and other axioms framed new directions in social entrepreneurship, sustainability, and diversity as a way to honor Punahou's dual debt to its missionary and Hawaiian benefactors.

Some might call this revisionist history, but the new stories drew on the school's past as

well. They brought previously overlooked facts into the spotlight and pulled characters from the wings of Punahou's history to center stage. What's more, Jim did not discard old stories, but told them alongside the new, with equal conviction. Sometimes the result was synthesis and new insight. Other times, old and new stories sat side by side uncomfortably, as if preparing for debate.

Whether synthesis or tension was the result, telling stories about Punahou in a new way began to shift the meaning behind many of Punahou's actions. Over time, it altered how faculty, staff, and students saw themselves and their school. "Jim's career has shifted what Punahou means to the world," says one faculty leader. "His narrative of this place is aspirational. It's better than who we are, but there's truth in it, and we're always striving to live up to that aspiration."

Jim's ability to weave distinct, even conflicting, storylines together extends from a lifetime of practice at bridging cultures and stitching threads of history into usable fabric. He was born and raised in Waimānalo, a rural, working-class, and predominantly Native Hawaiian community that was far—physically and figuratively—from Punahou School. Both his parents worked full time to support a household that was, as Jim describes it, "comfortable, but frugal." He and his brother Doug were admitted to Punahou in kindergarten.

His parents both worked for Hawaiian Telephone. His father started out selling ads in the Yellow Pages, worked his way up to sales, and eventually became a marketing executive. Jim's mother first worked as an operator and later trained others in the company. Their hard work and sacrifice paid two tuitions for 13 years, with the help of some financial aid from the school.

The student body of Punahou at the time was predominantly white, upper middle class, and from suburban East Honolulu. Yet, when asked if he ever felt set apart at Punahou, Jim recalls, "I never felt different. Generally, race, wealth, and neighborhood were not things we [students] cared about."

Clubs, sports, and the political geography of campus hangouts determined social affiliations. Jim was not the "Hawaiian kid from Waimānalo"—he was the quiet student, varsity baseball and basketball player, and, in his senior year, student body president.

There were certain occasions when differences in class or culture were evident—"like when a kid came to school driving a really nice car," says Jim, "or if you went to a classmate's house." There was also a time in elementary school Jim remembers vividly: "I always had to wait until five-thirty for my mom to pick me up when she got off work. I asked her why she couldn't come

President Scott, his wife, Maureen Dougherty '71, and their two children, Tessa '16 and Buddy '18, reside in the President's Home on the slopes of Rocky Hill. Built in 1907, the home stands as an example of island grace and hospitality. While the circular lānai was originally designed to be open to the Mānoa breezes, a 1984 renovation enclosed the lānai and added an attached pavilion to accommodate the many school events held here each year.

Arthur F. Griffiths, with his wife, Helen, and daughter, Eleanor (1925), was the first president to live in the home. He led Punahou from 1902 to 1922. Oliver G. Traphagen, the home's architect, worked in Honolulu during the early 1900s and designed the Moana, Waikīkī's first major hotel, completed in 1901.

31

to pick me up right after school like the other moms." Her succinct explanation: "'So we can pay for your tuition.'"

When Jim was admitted to Stanford University, a new set of bridging experiences began. He transitioned smoothly from island to continental culture, spending more than twenty years on the mainland, and earning degrees from prestigious universities on each coast—a BA from Stanford and an EdD from Harvard. He then took a position as headmaster of Catlin Gabel School in Portland, Oregon.

Jim's personal story took a new turn when his father passed away and he returned to the islands. "My dad never knew his birth father," he explains. "He was hānai to Leslie Scott, the second husband of his grandmother. Early on, he decided that Scott was going to be his name— James Liloa Purdy might have been his birth father, but he was a Scott. And from an early age, he told my brother and me, 'I can't leave you with much money, but I can leave you with a great education and a last name—Scott.'"

Because his father identified with his hānai family rather than his birth family, Jim's knowledge of his own native ancestry was limited. Moving back to Hawai'i to take the job of Punahou president helped change that. "In his later years my dad mellowed, and when he knew his days were short, he encouraged my brother and me to reach out to the Purdy side. When he passed, his half-sister, who had studied our lineage, took us through and substantiated and documented our Hawaiian side going all the way back to Kamehameha. I had been told that growing up, but I had never seen it documented.

"When I came back home to take this job, I made an effort to connect with the Purdy side of my family." Jim explored his ancestry while shaping a new vision for Punahou. The timing was fortuitous. "I've always gone back to story—to history—at transition points," he says. "I assume that whenever you're initiating change, story is going to be important because it gives people meaning—it gives people the 'why' of change. And it creates continuity for people, a way to connect new things with the past."

In early 2014, Pat Basset, the retired head of the National Association of Independent Schools (NAIS), spent a week at Punahou watching the school at work and sharing observations with faculty and administrators. For more than a decade Pat had led the NAIS, an organization with 1,700 member schools, including the nation's most prestigious college preparatory institutions. Near the end of his visit, I asked Pat what stood out about Punahou compared to the hundreds

of schools he'd visited over the years. "It's remarkable that a school as old and established as Punahou has been able to consistently innovate over the years," he said. "That will be one of the principal challenges going forward—how can it keep innovating, especially as its success and recognition grow? I'd also ask, 'Where does this capacity for continual innovation come from?'"

Punahou reaches back to the legend of Kapunahou for its own answers to this question. The "new spring" is invoked again and again in annual reports and archival documents to describe the school's ability to adapt, buck complacency, and embrace new ideas. Historically, the metaphor has connoted renewal rather than innovation, but, as Jim points out, "the Latin root of innovation, *innovatus*, means 'to renew.' There is continual renewal here."

When asked if Punahou's habit of innovation influenced him as a student, Jim reflects, "I couldn't point to specific things, but I saw it in my teachers. Even after I graduated, I remember teachers going on sabbatical—Bob Torrey, Doc Berry, Win Healy. Doc came back [and] reinvented himself, brought economics to the curriculum. Win introduced the variable schedule. It always seemed like teachers had the autonomy and freedom to try new things."

In 2004, after ten years as president, Jim presented the Punahou trustees with an unusual request. Following the example set by his teachers, he says, "I told the trustees I wanted to take some time to consider whether I should be around for another ten years." He asked for a month-long sabbatical at the Klingenstein Center, Teachers College, Columbia University—a program for leaders of independent and international schools. He would take time to consider whether and why to embark upon a second decade as president.

In his postsabbatical letter to the board, Jim said he looked forward to continuing his work at Punahou, provided he could devote twenty percent of his time to "public purpose" initiatives. "I needed the board to agree that it was important." They did.

Thereafter, Punahou pushed new initiatives, including the Clarence T. C. Ching PUEO (Partnerships in Unlimited Educational Opportunities) Program—now a nationally respected program offering summer classes and year-round academic mentoring to public-school students with high promise and limited economic opportunity. Other projects included the Luke Center for Public Service and an aggressive expansion of financial aid.

The notion that renewal is essential to excellence is widely held at Punahou. It is part of a leadership culture fostered by Jim and two of his closest instructional collaborators, Kevin Conway, Academy (9–12) principal, and Mike Walker, Junior School (K–8) principal.

Kevin came to Punahou in 2000, from the American School Foundation in Mexico City.

One of his early observations was that "we were holding teachers accountable for professional growth, but we could do more to help them grow." He sought the help of Assistant Principal Paula Hodges and a professional development committee composed of faculty, and together they created the Haku initiative.

Every five years, Academy teachers get a "Haku year," for which they design a course of professional development focused on one area of their craft. Teachers in their Haku year develop areas of focus with their department head, and create a plan for their own professional development. At the conclusion of a Haku year, teachers share what they've learned with colleagues. The school first offered the program to those faculty who were most skeptical about the concept. Once it had proved its value to them, the idea took off. "Now it's wildly popular," says one faculty member. "Every teacher asks, 'When is my Haku year?'"

During tough economic times, professional development is often the first thing schools cut back on, but Punahou increased its efforts in this area during the Great Recession of 2008. "We're fortunate to have the resources and institutional commitment to invest in professional development," says Kevin. That investment pays multiple dividends for Punahou, keeping instruction on the cutting edge while also attracting and retaining teachers with a passion for continuous improvement.

Emily McCarren, a former Academy faculty member and now the director of the Wo International Center, recalls of her hiring: "My interview was pretty standard. The first thing that really struck me was that the summer before I started, Paula and Kevin sent out a reading list and study questions to faculty. It included new research about effective instruction, and it opened this whole dialogue before the year even began. That's when I knew—this is a thoughtful place, a place where people are devoted to mastering their craft." Now, after years of working at Punahou, she says, "This is an amazing place to teach for anyone who wants to be a better teacher."

While investments in human capital were transforming the Academy, a physical and instructional transformation was underway in the Junior School. Mike Walker came to Punahou with a track record of reinvention. Like Kevin, Mike began his career at the American School Foundation in Mexico City, and then moved to leadership positions at US schools. He took over as headmaster of the Hammond School in Columbia, South Carolina, during a time of fiscal and organizational upheaval, within five years building a thriving school enhanced with opportunities for global learning and unique learning activities outside the traditional

overleaf

The President's Home serves as a gathering place to celebrate milestones during the school year—welcoming new faculty and staff, extending thanks to parents, celebrating student accomplishments, and hosting alumni during Reunion Week. In 2011, the Scotts hosted a dinner at the President's Home for world leaders visiting Hawai'i for the Asia-Pacific Economic Cooperation conference.

The grandfather clock was made by Uldrick Thompson from solid koa in the early 1900s. It is a gift from Harriet Castle (1859–65) Coleman, for whom the clock was originally crafted. Uldrick Thompson was a teacher and principal at Kamehameha School for Boys.

The koa cabinet may have been in the house for nearly a hundred years. Displayed on its shelves are documents associated with the Hawaiian Kingdom, including the first printed constitution and laws of the Hawaiian Islands, as well as early Hawaiian-language books, all from the Punahou Archives.

A 1917 photograph of the interior of the President's Home includes this cabinet. It was likely made by German cabinetmaker Wilhelm Fischer, who worked in Honolulu from 1850 to 1875. A master woodworker, Fischer became the royal cabinetmaker for Kings Kamehameha IV, Kamehameha V, and Kalākaua. His pieces are in the collections of 'Iolani Palace and Queen Emma Summer Palace.

classroom. He then moved to Vanderbilt University's Family-School Partnership Lab, where he orchestrated a similarly dramatic transformation.

Mike took the job of K–8 principal at Punahou in 1998. That year, he recalls, "At Carnival, Jim is walking with Steve Case ['76, former chairman and CEO of America Online], and Steve says, 'I'd like to do something to honor my parents.'" The work of planning what would become the Case Middle School began soon thereafter.

Mike's position involved him immediately in the project; his experience made him central to design and fundraising. "Jim and I made 152 presentations on Case Middle. He would speak to the strength of Punahou—the enrollment, the endowment, the faculty, the benchmarks of a thriving school. I would talk about the educational possibilities—how program was inseparable from facilities, how we were designing the space to optimize teaching and learning. That was the spring of my first year."

Mike has played a critical role in Punahou's physical transformation. He has been Jim's partner in facilities design and fund-raising, making scores of presentations to donors, trustees, and other stakeholders for the Omidyar K–1 Neighborhood. He has also been involved in the planning process for the new 2–5 Neighborhood, which will replace the aging Mary Persis Winne Elementary Units.

Like Kevin, Mike has led instructional renewal. He hired nearly half the Junior School faculty. "When you've been around long enough, that's bound to happen," he says. But the qualities that Punahou is looking for have changed during his tenure. The school is hiring teachers who are "innovators and collaborators," he says, and who are open to rooting instruction in research. "The way to improve instruction is to understand learning at its neurological foundation. We need to be a place that can marry research and practice."

Consistent with this emphasis, Punahou launched Professional Programs at Punahou, offering professional development to teachers from public and private schools across Hawai'i. The program helps teachers "become reflective practitioners, researchers, scholars, and authors" and "bridge the worlds of theory and practice…within the context of an innovative K–12 school." Professional Programs includes a summer Brain Symposium that helps teachers incorporate the latest brain science into teaching and curriculum; a Global Education Teacher Strand (workshops focused on designing globally focused curriculum); and a summer Lab School where cohorts of teachers observe classrooms, and then create lesson plans and activities for their own classes.

Jim's vision of where Professional Programs might lead is far-reaching. "Punahou should

be its own graduate school of education, like a university lab school—a place where research and practice inform each other." A Punahou graduate school offering advanced degrees would serve dual needs, he says: "It would help us develop our own talent, and a graduate school is a way to share with others," allowing teachers at public and private schools to benefit from Punahou's most valuable asset—its intellectual capital.

Jim expresses a thoughtful excitement as he talks about the possibility of a graduate school. It's obvious that new ideas fuel him—but he returns to history and narrative as touchstones, drawing on old stories to inform the new. "It would bring Oahu College back," he says, noting that the missionaries once envisioned Punahou as a postsecondary institution.

Even when he's imagining the future, Jim remains mindful of the past. "I didn't bring innovation to Punahou, it's why I came. Both my predecessors were president for about 25 years," he says. "I can see now how someone is able to stay in this job for that long. You have the chance to reinvent yourself because Punahou is always reinventing itself."

In 2008, William Damon, the director of the Stanford Center on Adolescence, published *The Path to Purpose*, a book based on his landmark four-year nationwide study of how young people find their purpose in life. Gathering data on thousands of young people ages 12 to 26, Damon found that "only one-fifth of young people today are thriving—highly engaged in activities they love and developing a clear sense of what they want to do with their lives." He found a majority "living at home longer, lacking career motivation, struggling to make a timely transition into adulthood," even after college.

Not surprisingly, he concluded that adults largely create the problem by investing too heavily in short-term benchmarks for youth—passing the test, graduating, making the grade or the team—and too little in questions of purpose: "What kind of person do I wish to become? What do I want to accomplish with my life? Why should I strive?" The result, he said, is a generation of young people adept at striving for near-term gains, but lacking the ability to set their own course.

So the question remains: Do Punahou graduates fare better than other young people, and have changes at Punahou over the past 25 years served them well in this regard? A conclusive answer would require a study approaching the scope of William Damon's book-length treatment. Lacking a research team and constrained by word count, I asked Jim what feedback he has heard from recent graduates.

Whenever Jim travels, he makes an effort to connect with alumni in order to ask, "What could Punahou have done better?" On one trip to San Francisco, he met with a group of newly minted alumni from Bay Area colleges. As the gathering was wrapping up, a young woman from the University of San Francisco spoke. "I wish Punahou had prepared us better for hapa issues," she said.

"People on the mainland see me as Asian," she went on to explain, "but I'm hapa. And I don't see myself in terms of race—that's not what defines me." Other alumni quickly chimed in with their own experiences of confronting a culture that put them in race-based boxes of identity—a surprise to islanders from multiethnic Hawai'i. The conversation between Jim and the alumni stretched an hour past its scheduled time.

This anecdote provided clues to the postgraduation experience, but, needing more information, I reached out to as many recent grads as I could. Some I knew through friends or family. Others I'd met as juniors and seniors through the Entrepreneurs in Residence (EIR) Program at the Luke Center for Public Service, which pairs mentors from the community with students working on group projects with community impact. Though my sampling was far from representative, the alumni who responded had all gone on to four-year college and ranged in age from 20 to 28. Some were still in school, while others were beginning their work life.

By and large, these alumni were doing remarkable things and had a clear sense of purpose. An engineering major at Princeton was completing a summer internship spent designing water systems in developing countries; a recent college graduate was setting up microloans to small farmers in order to build a more sustainable food supply; a young entrepreneur who'd moved home after college was expanding his successful business; one woman was doing her medical residency at a prestigious hospital; a senior manager in renewable energy was climbing through the company ranks; and another woman was combining her experience in teaching and start-ups to support women in the male-dominated world of technology.

Some alumni who'd only recently entered college already knew what direction they desired and attributed that certainty to Punahou. "From my first day [at Harvard]," said one alumnus, a second-year university student, "I've dedicated much of my time to public service. I volunteer at the country's oldest student-run homeless shelter, serve as a mentor to a local high-school student, and became an officer in the Phillips Brooks House Association, which I like to think of as college-level Luke Leaders."

Another alumnus's comment pointed to a different, but no less direction-setting, value derived from Punahou: "The most important thing I learned from spending as much time as I did thinking about social entrepreneurship was that social entrepreneurship is not for me. I learned the importance I place on direct service instead. [Without Punahou] I doubt I would have been able to learn these things—about service, social entrepreneurship, and myself."

Some alumni offered suggestions about how Punahou could better help students find their calling, including this courageous insight: "I would challenge the school to move beyond the message of 'To whom much is given, much is expected.' I heard this message many times over my years, and it undoubtedly shaped my dedication to service. Attending Punahou is a privilege, but it should not be all that motivates us. Service to others must not be motivated by a sense of guilt or expectation, but by a recognition of the dignity of another."

These testimonials offered encouraging evidence of Punahou's impact upon its graduates and their life trajectory. They painted a picture of graduates actively pursuing their destinies, acknowledging Punahou's contribution while also looking back gratefully, critically, and analytically. But other comments revealed a pervasive anxiety, an uncertainty about the future, and a harried pursuit of life purpose.

"I'm applying to law school . . . I don't want to practice law—my passion is education. I'm hoping to find a way to use law to affect education."

"I'm still trying to pick a major—chemistry would keep me on a premed track, but I love psychology. Med school is probably the more practical course."

"I'm taking a job with a consulting firm for now. Eventually I want to start my own business. I need time to figure out what kind. Plus, it's a good way to develop business skills."

"I enjoy political science. I've thought about getting a PhD, but I don't know that I want to be a professor."

"After graduation, I'm going to teach English in Japan and use the time to figure out my next step."

Taken together, the comments of young alumni—both the confident and the undecided—reflect an exciting and unnerving mix of idealism and uncertainty. This may simply be an inevitable feature of young adulthood—the messy work of forging identity, finding purpose, and managing change. It may also reflect the inevitable crisis of identity as one moves from the islands to the wider world, and from youth to adulthood.

Interpreted another way, though, the struggles of these graduates in their twenties may point to a new opportunity for reinvention at Punahou. For the past 25 years, change at Punahou has been rooted in an ethic of personal renewal and powerful narratives of identity and purpose. Leaders at Punahou are brimming with skill and experience in initiating and managing transformation. Jim Scott himself is a master at driving change—both personal and institutional—through meaningful stories that inspire resolve.

The mix of anxiety and aspiration in these young people may portend a future body of work at Punahou, one that calls upon the school's leaders to pass on their expertise in transformation to students—preparing graduates to craft their own moving life stories, rewrite old plots when they wear thin, and unify narrative fragments of life into a purposeful whole—just as the school's faculty and administrators have done in their own lives and work.

Punahou would serve future graduates well by teaching them the art of constructing meaningful stories of self from which to draw a powerful sense of identity and purpose. Equipped with this skill, graduates can forge a sense of themselves strong enough to withstand the narratives foisted upon them by others—by their peers, by society, even by Punahou itself. Then, through their character and accomplishments, they will rewrite the story of Punahou, just as its current president has done.

CONSTANCE HEE LAU 1970

BY SARA LIN '99

Dressed in a pink leotard and tights, an eleven-year-old Constance Hee bounded across the wooden floors of the Connors Dance Pavilion, raising her chin and sticking out her chest as her teacher, Josephine Flanders, cried out, "Accentuate the positive!"

Years later, that exclamation became a mantra for Constance Hee '70 Lau, who has become one of Hawai'i's most powerful businesswomen. With diplomas from Yale University, the University of California Hastings College of the Law, and Stanford University, she joined the Hawaiian Electric Company (HECO) in 1984 as assistant corporate counsel and quickly climbed through the ranks. By 2001, she was the president and CEO of American Savings Bank, and five years later she became the first female president and CEO of Hawaiian Electric Industries (HEI), the parent company of both HECO and American Savings Bank.

She's come a long way for a girl who grew up on Kāne'ohe Bay, back when the Windward coast felt as remote to Honolulu as Waialua feels today. She remembers her parents stopping along Old Pali Highway to cut long stalks of wild ginger with a machete for the family stewpot. Her father, a vaudeville performer turned real estate broker, was a fisherman at heart and fed the family off the

opposite
Constance Hee Lau at her childhood home on Kāne'ohe Bay

bay. He taught Lau to dig for clams and catch creamy white "7-11" crabs, named for the seven large red dots on their backs. In the afternoons during high tide, she and her father took nets into the water and made a circle, catching huge schools of mullet, ulua, and barracuda.

"I'm actually very good at cleaning fish," she says, chuckling as she recounts her self-described "country bumpkin" upbringing.

Living in the country had its downsides. "It was hard to get dates," she says, because parents wouldn't let their teenage boys drive all the way to the Windward side. She'd have to go to her aunt's house in town to meet dates.

Still, growing up in Kāne'ohe left an indelible—and positive—mark. Perhaps it was the hours spent lying on the lawn with her mom watching cloud shapes, or the times she caught bucketfuls of bufo toads for her high school science class to dissect. The latest brain research, which Punahou follows closely and incorporates into its curriculum, shows that growing up around nature helps children learn to think more creatively. Lau's experience confirms this—she has become a supreme problem solver.

In 1999, as a court-appointed special purpose trustee, Lau was tapped along with four other

Hawai'i leaders to help Kamehameha Schools through one of its most critical transitions. She took the lead in restructuring the Schools' investment policies in order to maintain its tax-exempt status.

"Connie, to me, was the single person that put Kamehameha Schools back on track to becoming financially stable," says former Kamehameha Schools trustee Robert Kihune. "She actually had to tutor us [the other trustees] about how to do investments, because we were thrown together just to solve a problem, but then we were interim trustees and had to run the school."

Facing crowds of impassioned and often angry Native Hawaiian families was part of the job, too. But Lau never lost her cool, Kihune says: "She had a calming effect. She's not the kind of person that wears her title. What you see is what you get."

For Lau, that meant conducting herself as a trustee as she does in business: with an open mind and open ears. "You have to be willing to really listen, because what you basically have to figure out is how to interact with all the different audiences and all the different constituencies," Lau says matter-of-factly. Throughout her term as interim trustee, she and her husband, Russell Lau '70, were busy raising three children: Jennifer '04, Gregory '06, and Eric '10.

She makes it sound easy, but that's part of her charm—she's modest about her talents. In addition to undertaking her CEO duties at HEI, Lau sits on the boards of more than a dozen nonprofits and serves as a Punahou School trustee.

As the head of HEI, Lau is in charge of moving the utility away from its traditional oil-fired generators toward renewable sources of energy. The state-mandated Hawai'i Clean Energy Initiative calls for achieving one hundred percent clean energy by 2045, to be achieved through energy efficiency and alternative renewable energy sources, including solar, wind, geothermal, and biofuel. Some have criticized HEI for moving too slowly on the long-term goals of the Initiative, but HECO is ahead of its 2015 renewable energy goals. Meanwhile, a merger proposal from Florida-based Next-Era Energy, Inc. has generated strong debate as regulatory processes unfold.

Lau embraces the challenges and complexities of change, drawing inspiration from those indelible early lessons. "I don't think in terms of failing." she says. "You have to think extremely positively. That dance piece, 'Accentuate the positive,' I try to live by that."

NAINOA THOMPSON 1972

BY DAVIANNA PŌMAIKA'I MCGREGOR

Nainoa Thompson '72 is the most celebrated of the first generation of Native Hawaiians since AD 1400 to master the Polynesian art of non-instrument ocean navigation, or wayfinding. His importance comes into focus when one recalls that, following the overthrow of the Hawaiian monarchy and the start of governance of Hawai'i as a territory of the United States, Native Hawaiian national and cultural identity diminished. Though Hawaiians took pride in the legendary intentional voyages their ancestors made throughout the more than 60 million square miles of the Pacific Ocean, those achievements remained in the distant past—that is, until the Polynesian Voyaging Society successfully re-created the ancestral voyages in the 1970s and 1980s in its double-hulled voyaging canoe, the *Hōkūle'a*. The *Hōkūle'a* reinstilled national pride in our generation of Native Hawaiians—a pride we have passed on to the next generation—and served as a catalyst for the brilliant renaissance of Hawaiian culture, language, and science.

At the forefront of these voyages was Nainoa Thompson, who is inextricably linked with the achievements of the *Hōkūle'a* and its epic journeys throughout the Pacific and the world. People compose songs and chants in his honor, name their

The wind's blowing, there are no stars showing
Nainoa's navigating, hold on tight.
Raise the island Tutuila
Pago Pago's in sight
Sail on and on and on
Like a bird in flight

opposite
Hōkūle'a *sailing along the northern coast of Moloka'i, bound for Kalaupapa, 1997*

children after him, and regard him as the most widely known and trusted Native Hawaiian leader today.

Mo'okū'auhau (genealogies) connect contemporary Native Hawaiians with our ancestors and with each other as a people within our national and cultural homeland, Hawai'i. Through his mother, Laura Lucas '43 Thompson, Nainoa traces his genealogy to Keli'ikipikaneokalohaka, whose great-grandfather was Kamehameha I, the high chief of Hawai'i Island. Kamehameha united the islands of Hawai'i under one rule and founded the Hawaiian Kingdom.

Just as meaningful is the symbolic genealogy of those Nainoa considers his mentors in his roles as a beloved and honorable son, husband, father, learner, navigator, teacher, and leader. The humble and reserved Nainoa, admired for his seafaring accomplishments and sought after for his inspirational and visionary keynote addresses, conveys universal lessons to audiences by sharing how he learned his craft from his mentors. To gain an insight into the values and beliefs he has embraced and is transmitting to a new generation of navigators, I asked Nainoa to share the contributions of his principal guides in his life's journey.

Yoshio Kawano, a Nisei worker at his grand-

Ha'ina mai ka puana;
So the story is told
Hōkūle'a *sails the ocean highways*
With the family both young and old.

HŌKŪLE'A HULA

BY CARLOS ANDRADE

father's dairy, laid the foundation for Nainoa's life-long relationship with the ocean. He gave Nainoa his first fishing pole and would take Nainoa fishing after he finished delivering milk at 4:30 a.m. At Punahou School, two extraordinary teachers—fifth-grade teacher Mabel Hefty and football coach Charlie Ane '49—believed in Nainoa and encouraged him. In his own role as an educator, he is passing along the values, beliefs, and trust they imparted.

Through Punahou, Nainoa also formed an enduring friendship with fellow alumnus Lacy Veach '62, who served as the lead astronaut of robotics development and operation for the International Space Station before his death in 1995. The two often discussed their notion of navigating the future with the wisdom of the ancestors—aligning the power of science and technology with the values of traditional Hawaiian culture. These discussions inspired the Polynesian Voyaging Society's Mālama Honua Worldwide Voyage.

Nainoa's endeavors with the *Hōkūle'a* mirror the vision, courage, and determination of five inspirational men. Artist Herb Kawainui Kāne envisioned the canoe, and then designed and built it. Mau Piailug of Satawal, Yap, a grand master navigator, trained Nainoa as a navigator, taking him

opposite
Nainoa Thompson, carrying a sacred stone from Hawai'i to place at the ancient marae *of Taputapuātea in Ra'iātea, Tahiti. He stands behind Mau Piailug (left), Tava Taupu, and Myron "Pinky" Thompson. Punahou teacher Ka'aumoana McKenney '83 is at left rear. Taputapuātea was a place of learning for ancient Polynesian navigators, and canoes set out from this sacred* marae *to settle all parts of Polynesia.*

In 1962, Bishop Museum archaeologists Kenneth Emory (1916) and Yosihiko Sinoto initiated ground-breaking research at Taputapuātea on ancient Polynesian migrations. Sinoto, joined by his son Aki '69, later established a program of conservation and stabilization for the site.

In 1995, for the first time in centuries, canoes from Aotearoa, Rarotonga, Hawai'i, and Tahiti ceremonially entered Te Ava Mo'a, the pass into the lagoon associated with Taputapuātea. Each group placed a sacred stone from their home islands on the marae *to reaffirm and revitalize the bonds that unite Polynesia.*

through a window of time to connect to the realm of our Pacific ancestors. World-renowned surfer and all-around ocean man Eddie Aikau set a high bar—one that will challenge the next generation—with his courage, commitment, and love of the *Hōkūle'a*. When the *Hōkūle'a* capsized in treacherous seas 12 miles south of Moloka'i, Eddie embarked on a paddleboard to get help and was never seen again.

Nainoa credits his father, Myron Thompson '43,

and Will Kyselka, the head of the Bishop Museum's planetarium and the author of *An Ocean in Mind*, for steering himself and the Polynesian Voyaging Society through its most difficult period following the loss of Eddie Aikau. Nainoa has internalized the lessons of his mentors as a foundation for his own exceptional accomplishments—inspiring and training a new generation of navigators and sailing crews and spreading the message of mālama honua, the Hawaiian way of caring for, respecting, and honoring our Earth.

Like the chiefs known to have voyaged from Hawai'i to Kahiki and beyond, and then back again—including Kaulu, Hema, Mo'ikeha, Kila, and La'amaikahiki—Nainoa Thompson is honored and recognized for his vision, courage, leadership, and determination. He has played a central role in rediscovering the knowledge of our Hawaiian ancestors, who navigated their oceanic routes guided by the stars and natural elements—and, even more important, he has helped perpetuate that knowledge. Nainoa has reconnected Hawaiians with our Pacific Islands 'ohana and launched a worldwide voyage to carry the message of our collective responsibility to nurture and sustain the Earth's natural resources so that future generations may flourish.

opposite

Mamiya Science Center opened in January of 1999. Built in the same location as McNeil Hall, the previous science facility, the Center was designed to incorporate dramatic advances in the teaching of science. This visually open setting provides a laboratory environment for inquiry-based experiential learning for the exploration of biology, chemistry, and physics.

Designed by John Hara '57, and prominently situated on Chamberlain Drive, the Center includes Academy classrooms and laboratories, a workshop serving both the Junior School (K–8) and the Academy (9–12), a lecture hall, and faculty offices.

The Center is named for Punahou trustees Richard and Hazel Mamiya— he a respected heart surgeon, and she a tireless volunteer for Punahou and the community.

below

The power of science and technology, when wielded with the wisdom and values of a culture vitally connected to its environment, was a topic that astronaut Lacy Veach '62 and navigator Nainoa Thompson '72 discussed often. The friendship between Thompson and Veach—one an explorer of oceans, the other an explorer of outer space—blossomed into the Mālama Honua Worldwide Voyage. The notion of navigating the future with the wisdom of our Polynesian ancestors is expressed in the Mamiya Science Center mosaic, which was designed by Thompson to incorporate Mau Piailug's Micronesian star compass and the space shuttle's elliptical path around the Earth.

previous pages (pp. 52–53)
Home to grades nine to twelve, the Academy Quadrangle
is anchored by historic Cooke Hall (1909). The tamarind
tree shown on the far right (p. 53) next to Alexander
Hall is nearly as old as the school. The tree was planted
during the first year by a group of boys in a spot that
was then a courtyard of the 'E' building, Punahou's
first school structure.

opposite
William D. Alexander Hall with Mamiya Science
Center in the background. William DeWitt Alexander
(1842–49) was named the fourth president of Punahou
in 1864 (then called Oahu College). He was the first
alumnus to lead the school, and he later served as
a school trustee.

A historian and linguist, Alexander published
A Brief History of the Hawaiian Islands, and
Introduction to Hawaiian Grammar. He became
the first surveyor general of the Kingdom of Hawaii,
sat on the Board of Education from 1874 to 1895,
and became Commissioner of Public Instruction.
W. D. Alexander Hall, built in 1933, was designed
by architect Charles W. Dickey, who was
Alexander's nephew.

left
Rev. William P. Alexander and his wife,
Mary Ann McKinney, had nine children,
the eldest of whom was William DeWitt.
The Alexanders were stationed at Waiʻoli
on Kauaʻi (pp. iv–v) and then at Lahainaluna on Maui. Rev. Alexander recalled in
his memoir the excitement that accompanied the youngsters' return to Lahaina at
the end of the Punahou School term.

"The home-coming of these children,…
in small, slow-sailing craft, was a great
event at Lahainaluna. A white flag at
the mast-head, the usual signal of
missionaries, or of their children,
announced their coming…The time
of vacations passed quickly for the
children, in baths in the sea, rambles
in the valley, and excursions to the
summits in the mountains."

below
In the nineteenth century, small boys
were dressed in gowns or dresses, and
this portrait shows W. D. Alexander's son,
Arthur (1883), at about three years of age
in the mid-1860s. He grew up at Punahou
during his father's tenure as school president, and later worked as a surveyor for
Alexander & Baldwin, Ltd., the company
founded by his uncles, Samuel T. Alexander (1842–60) and Henry P. Baldwin
(1847–63).

The Alexanders considered Punahou a
beloved family project and Arthur served
as a school trustee from 1910 to 1945.
He played a key role in the construction
of Samuel T. Alexander Field (1908) and in
working with New York architect Bertram
Goodhue on the campus master plan.

This 1819 copy of Memoirs of Henry Obookiah belonged to Lucy Thurston, wife of Rev. Asa Thurston, who may have brought it on her 164-day voyage from Boston to Kailua-Kona in 1820. ʻŌpūkahaiʻa, born in Kaʻū in 1792, was one of several Hawaiian youths educated by missionaries in Connecticut. He converted to Christianity, became an avid evangelist, and began working on a grammar for the Hawaiian language. Before he could return to Hawaiʻi to preach, he contracted typhus fever and died in 1818 at the age of twenty-six.

His religious zeal and love for Hawaiʻi and its people inspired the ABCFM to send a contingent of missionaries to the Sandwich Islands in 1820. His remains were brought back to Hawaiʻi Island from Cornwall, Connecticut, by his family in 1993.

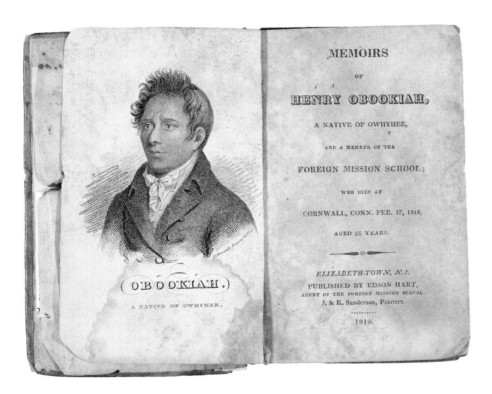

MEMOIRS

OF

HENRY OBOOKIAH,

A NATIVE OF OWHYHEE,

AND A MEMBER OF THE

FOREIGN MISSION SCHOOL;

WHO DIED AT

CORNWALL, CONN. FEB. 17, 1818,

AGED 26 YEARS.

ELIZABETH-TOWN, N.J.
PUBLISHED BY EDSON HART,
AGENT OF THE FOREIGN MISSION SCHOOL.
J. & E. Sanderson, Printers.
1819.

OBOOKIAH.

A NATIVE OF OWHYHEE.

Alexander Hall is flanked by Cooke Hall (shown here on the right) and Cooke Library. Rare books and a rich collection of photographs, published and unpublished documents, artifacts, and original art related to the school's storied history are part of the Punahou Archives located in Cooke Library. The Library also includes Kirsch Art Gallery, an extensive multimedia collection, Sony-Morita Language Lab, and a writing center that primarily serve Academy students and faculty. Cooke Library was designed by architect Ernest Hara '28 and completed in 1965; Hara served as a Punahou School trustee from 1969 to 1985.

In 1995, the Punahou Archives received a collection of stamping dies from Honolulu jewelers Hildgund at Dawkins Benny, which included medals, rings, and jewelry associated with the school during the early 1900s. The selection includes dies for the Oahu College Athletic Association featuring the Winged O, the Punahou Academy Girls Athletic Association with a stylized P, and the Punahou Invitational Relays. Founded in 1946, the Punahou Invitational Relays is the state's longest-running high school track-and-field event.

59

In June 1866 the school celebrated the
25th anniversary of its 1841 founding.
About 150 people gathered at Old School
Hall for the quarter-century celebration.

Today, more than 3,000 alumni return
to the campus during Alumni Week each
June following commencement. The focal
point is the Alumni Lūʻau hosted by the
24th Reunion Class and held on Rice
Field adjacent to the spring. The copper-
clad pyramid roof of Thurston Chapel
quietly emphasizes the geographical
and spiritual center of the school—
Kapunahou—the natural spring
after which the school is named.

Before the start of the Lūʻau, President
Jim Scott and Maureen Dougherty Scott
host the 50th Reunion Class at a cocktail
reception at the President's Home overlooking the campus. Here, following the
reception, Jim and Maureen lead the
50th Reunion Class of 1964 in the
procession to the Lūʻau.

At the school's centennial in 1941, the Hawaiian Historical Society presented this plaque commemorating the generosity of the chiefs who gifted Kapunahou—Kaʻahumanu, Hoapili, Liliha, and Boki. The plaque was designed, modeled, and cast at the J. B. Castle School of Manual Arts at Punahou; the stone on which it is mounted was presented by the Kamehameha Schools. Delayed by the intervening war years, the dedication was held in 1951 with President John Fox presiding.

At the dedication, ʻIolani Luahine, one of the most important practitioners of traditional hula in the twentieth century, presented a chant in honor of the spring. Author and educator Ethel M. Damon (1901) told the story of early Punahou.

opposite

Kameʻeiamoku and his son, Hoapili, were members of Kamehameha's court, which in the early 1800s, moved from Waikīkī to the harbor at Honolulu. In this new center of commercial and political power, Kamehameha lived within an enclosure that included Kaʻahumanu's large grass house. This lithograph, made from an 1816 drawing by Louis Choris, shows the chiefs' compound, Kamehameha's Fort Kekuanohu and fleet, as well as foreign vessels. Today's Fort Street is named after this early coral-block structure. The extended households of the chiefs consisted of more than 2,000 people living in grass houses along the shoreline from Nuʻuanu Stream to Kakaʻako.

Rev. Asa and Lucy Goodale Thurston were part of the first company of missionaries to arrive in Hawai'i in 1820. Based in Kailua-Kona, Asa Thurston directed the construction of the present Moku'aikaua Church, the oldest Christian church in Hawai'i.

Before Punahou was established, missionary families shared study books. In his reminiscences published in 1916, Sereno Bishop recalled being sent to the Thurstons with books before daylight, "I found the three Thurstons at their lessons, seated at a table built around a post in the center of the sitting room. They were using a tallow candle, which was a novelty to me. Each one was enveloped in a large tapa, after the manner of the natives in cool weather."

Rev. Thurston was a founding trustee of Punahou School, and the school's Asa Thurston Physical Education Center is named in his honor. Lucy was much admired by Queen Lili'uokalani, whom she described in the manuscript of her 1895 autobiography as "...a woman of the greatest determination and of extraordinary strength of character." She went on to note that Lucy's grandson, Lorrin Andrews Thurston (1872–75), "comes rightfully by his determination"— he played a prominent role in the 1893 overthrow of the Hawaiian Kingdom and the subsequent establishment of the Republic of Hawaii.

Rev. Lorenzo Lyons, a founding trustee of Punahou School, is perhaps best known today as the lyricist for "Hawai'i Aloha," the oft-sung hymn expressing love for Hawai'i. He was an eloquent preacher, a prolific writer, and a strong proponent of the Hawaiian language.

For fifty-four years, Rev. Lyons was in charge of ministering to the largest mission station in the islands— Kawaihae to Hāmākua on the island of Hawai'i. He and Lucia Garratt Smith, his second wife, lived in Waimea, their base being 'Imiola Church, one of fourteen churches built under his tutelage. He was kind, devoted, and greatly loved by his parishioners.

HAWAI'I ALOHA

E Hawai'i e ku'u one hānau e
Ku'u home kulaīwi nei
'Oli nō au i nā pono lani ou
E Hawai'i, aloha ē

HUI

E hau'oli nā 'ōpio o Hawai'i nei
'Oli ē! 'Oli ē!
Mai nā aheahe makani e pā mai nei
Mau ke aloha, no Hawai'i

E ha'i mai kou mau kini lani e
Kou mau kupa aloha, e Hawai'i
Nā mea 'ōlino kamaha'o no luna mai
E Hawai'i, aloha ē

Nā ke Akua E mālama mai iā 'oe
Kou mau kualona aloha nei
Kou mau kahawai 'ōlinolino mau
Kou mau māla pua nani ē

Rev. Peter and Fanny Thomas Gulick were stationed in Koloa, Kaua'i, but with the establishment of Punahou School in 1841, Mrs. Gulick and seven of her eight children moved to Honolulu. Oldest son, Luther, had been shipped off from Kaua'i to New England for schooling in 1840 at age twelve, leaving his mother ill with the parting. He reached New England after an eight-month voyage, having served part of the way as cabin boy.

On the opening day of school in 1842, Charles and William walked to Punahou over the barren Honolulu plain from their rented house. Orramel and John were already settled in as boarders. Rev. Dole, principal, described the seven rooms for boarders within the E-Building, "As a general thing, two children occupy one room. He will need a bed & all the appurtenances, including a musketoe [mosquito] netting. There should be in the room a table, or desk, 3 or 4 chairs & a mirror, also a wash stand & what is necessary for ablutions."

Rev. Gulick was a Punahou trustee when the school received its charter in 1849. His son, Luther was a school trustee from 1865 to 1870.

Architect Vladimir Ossipoff insightfully chose the site of the legendary spring to build Thurston Memorial Chapel. Completed in late 1966 and dedicated in early 1967, Thurston Chapel was a gift to Punahou School from Robert S. (1906) and Evelyn Thurston in honor of their only child, Robert Jr. '41. The chapel walls are constructed just inside the rim of the pond, allowing water to flow into the chapel interior. On the mauka side of the chapel, adjacent to a landscaped courtyard, the Luke Center for Public Service adds to this oasis of serenity. Luke Center, a gift from the K. J. Luke Family, opened in 2004.

This modern complex encompasses the founders' ethic of combining spiritual practice and public service. Robert Shipman Thurston Jr. '41, was the great-great-grandson of Rev. Asa and Lucy Thurston.

PUBLIC PURPOSE

MARY VORSINO

opposite

Four pairs of koa entrance doors set within the simple, whitewashed, exterior walls of Thurston Memorial Chapel feature thirty-two copper panels, each depicting a scene from the life of Christ. Artist Jean Charlot designed the panels after considering suggestions from Punahou students. The copper repoussé panels were sculpted by artist Evelyn Giddings. This display begins with the Annunciation to the Virgin Mary and ends with young Jesus among the doctors in the temple.

They gather in an open-air garden shed just outside the state-funded Next Step homeless shelter in Kakaʻako, and prepare their lesson materials atop a stack of wooden pallets. On this Saturday morning, this is their classroom. It's where they'll be teaching a big concept—food self-sufficiency—and it's where they'll be learning some big concepts, too, about friendship and mentorship, about citizenship and service. The group—six Punahou School students, all members of the class of 2014—begin to welcome children from the shelter who are trickling their way over in twos and threes, hair still wet from their morning baths. The students beckon the kids closer, and before long they're holding hands and giving hugs.

The seniors are here to demonstrate how hydroponics works—and to show kids who might not have much access to fresh produce that a garden can take up very little space and yet yield big results. They tell me the project grew out of a desire to *do something*: The students delved into the issue of food insecurity during an intensive summer leadership program at Punahou, and decided to explore it with a real-world project as part of their required service learning course for seniors. So they came up with a plan: They would grow a hydroponics garden with homeless children, returning to Next Step every few weeks to track the progress of the plants and teach new concepts.

Today's lesson begins with planting. The children gingerly drop lettuce seeds into little hydroponic containers, and then get instructions on how to care for their mini-garden. Once the formal lesson is over, the group moves to an open area of asphalt to play. Two teens hoist the younger kids on their backs and whiz them around; another crouches down in front of a quieter child and speaks to her in a whisper. There is giggling and shouting. One of the Punahou seniors, Issei Funatsu '14, says the service project is about sharing something tangible that could make a difference for a family in need. But, he adds, he doesn't think he's giving as much as he's getting. "By coming here, we actually understand what the real problems are in society," he says. "Watching the kids growing up and becoming a mentor, it's what I've been very happy to do."

Public service has long had a home at Punahou. Teachers have brought it into their classrooms with projects big and small, from canned food drives to beach cleanups to fundraisers. Since the 1980s, seniors have been required to take a community service course. And year after year, in their sermons and their mentorship, Punahou chaplains have talked about the incredible power of a helping hand and an open heart.

But the public service happening on Punahou's campus today is more mature, more intentional, and connected to a broader school-wide mission to serve as a philanthropic and community-minded institution that instills the power of public good in its students—and whose positive impact extends far beyond the school's walls. Through new funding, new focus, and new programs, Punahou administrators, faculty, alumni, and supporters have fundamentally shifted the role of one of Hawai'i's most prestigious private schools—advancing it from an institution that delivers a world-class education to one that also serves the public good.

Modern Punahou has sought to forge new connections with community organizations, giving students the chance to help people in lasting ways; it has launched programs that offer enrichment, instruction, and pathways to college for hundreds of public-school students who have never contemplated the Punahou admissions process or paid tuition; it has sought to give Punahou students, like those in the Next Step hydroponics group, new experiences that will help them begin to see the problems at their front door—and then think through new ways to address them.

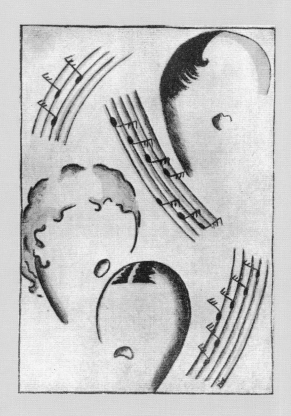

Punahou fuses public service with its curriculum and instruction rather than leaving the inclusion of philanthropy to accident or to the initiative of individual educators. This approach is not only about instilling caring and compassion in students—it's about urgently seeking for solutions to society's biggest challenges. "Part of Punahou's mission is developing social responsibility among our kids," says President Jim Scott, who has led the school since 1994. "Students create a community with one another that becomes a gift. My message to them is, you don't repay it, you pay it forward by making another life better, by helping another person reach their aspirations."

Scott's push to situate public purpose as central to Punahou's identity grew in large part out of disappointment in his own experiences as a student at the school. When he graduated in 1970, he was grateful for the educational preparation and the quality of instruction, but felt that something fundamental was missing. By creating an insulated community that existed only on the school's campus—76 acres in Mānoa Valley—Punahou, he thought, had neglected to ensure that he connected with, and made a difference in, his own community. "It's dangerous for any private school to be isolated from its community," Scott says. "You're not doing a service to kids; you're not doing a service to parents."

So when Scott returned to Punahou 24 years later as its president, after having served at private schools in the continental United States, he wanted to make sure students weren't just building a community on campus, but were getting to know, understand, and improve the one beyond the school, too. He wanted to build a private school with a public purpose.

When Scott talks about Punahou's public service mission at commencement ceremonies, at open houses, and in conversations with parents, he often uses a familiar phrase: "To whom much is given, much is expected." He remembers hearing similar words (paraphrased from the Book of Luke) during his own years at Punahou. By using them he's reminding Punahou's community—on campus as well as in the broader world—that public service was never a foreign concept at the school, even if it might not always have been so front and center as it has become under his leadership.

Indeed, many alumni and faculty point out that Punahou's founders sought to improve their community by building a school that would offer high-quality educational experiences. And, Scott notes, when he took the school's helm it already *had* an active public service agenda. Punahou required its seniors to perform community service, and projects were happening across the school, in classrooms and in after-school programs. Public service has always had a place at Punahou, he says: "I think a lot of graduates have felt that way. But I don't think it was a top-of-mind, explicit message."

The evolution of public service at Punahou has not only expanded opportunities for student community projects—it has prompted the school's leaders to continually ask: What are *we* doing to make the world a better place? Administrators have sought to answer that question with a growing list of initiatives and programs. The school has bolstered financial aid. It has built an on-campus center designed to plan, support, and enrich service-focused learning experiences for students. And it has launched or broadened a range of community programs, including the Student Global Leadership Institute (SGLI), an intensive summer program that invites students from across the globe to tackle a pressing topic, and the Clarence T. C. Ching PUEO (Partnerships in Unlimited Educational Opportunities) Program, an acclaimed college preparation and support program for low-income public-school students.

Punahou administrators have acknowledged a tension that surfaces in all this growth: Some parents and members of the community argue that the school would do better to spend its time and money on bolstering academic programs, expanding facilities, hiring more faculty members, or meeting any of a plethora of other school needs. The Wo International Center is expanding its public offerings for students and teachers, including language classes open to public-school students. Emily McCarren, the center's director, says the burden is on Punahou to show why a school with a public purpose is beneficial for all—teachers, students, parents, and the community. Serving Punahou students and serving the community can't and shouldn't be seen as mutually exclusive endeavors, she adds: "A school that is committed to having a public purpose becomes inherently a richer learning environment."

Punahou's work to bolster its public service mission and programming comes amid a national conversation about the role of private educational institutions, and about the importance of giving students not only the academic fundamentals required to succeed in life, but a moral and ethical compass, a sense of empathy and of right and wrong, and a desire to find solutions that will benefit mankind. Teaching public service at Punahou, administrators and faculty say, is not just about helping the community. It's about helping its students, about giving them mentally challenging, hands-on experiences where they're able to apply what they've learned, survey the landscape, understand real-world problems, and walk in the shoes of others. All this, Scott says, "is part of our mission of getting our kids ready not just for college, but for life."

You shouldn't be a burden to those you're trying to help ⁓

There's a whiteboard in Carri Morgan's office with hardly any white space on it. It's crammed with short descriptions, written in black, green, and blue marker, of active public service projects at Punahou: things happening in classrooms or clubs, things happening after school, events with younger kids and older ones. The initiatives include food and clothing drives, visits to senior homes, and projects that promote composting, wind energy, and literacy. The list is almost too much to keep track of, and it's always growing.

As the director of the Luke Center for Public Service, Morgan's central objective is to help bring service learning projects to fruition, whether they're incorporated into classroom lessons, part of campus-wide initiatives, or the work of small groups of students working after school and on weekends. All the work is designed to give students a greater understanding of the problems the community is facing, and how to tackle them (in small ways and big ones). "The idea is to educate the brain, the heart, and the hands of our students," Morgan says. "It's to help them know and understand what their responsibility is for making another life better."

Punahou founded the Luke Center in 2004, thanks to lead funding from the K. J. Luke Foundation, modeling it after collegiate programs such as the Haas Center for Public Service at Stanford University. When Punahou launched the Luke Center, it held a unique position as the nation's first service learning center, with a building and staff, on a K–12 private school campus. Punahou teachers embraced it, seeing the center as a way to make public service projects more meaningful and transformative. Morgan says her job isn't to co-opt teachers' public

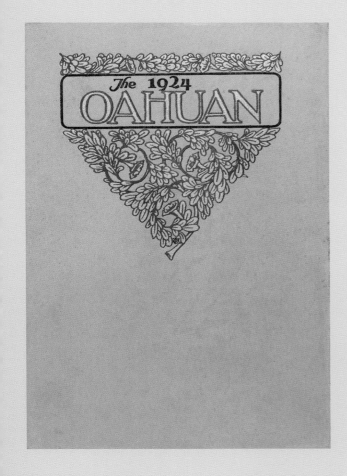

service efforts or dictate how they happen. Rather, she assists teachers in broadening those efforts —in making them fuller, more enriching, and more thoughtful.

Morgan's work is multifaceted: She reaches out to nonprofits. She facilitates drives, events, and field trips. She works with teachers to help them incorporate service learning into their curricula. And she gives presentations to classrooms to help students connect what they're learning—about homelessness, environmental sustainability, or food insecurity, for example— and what they're doing, whether they're raising money for a charity, collecting canned food, or planting gardens at homeless shelters.

The center also makes connections with community organizations to better understand their needs and how Punahou's service learning projects might address them. Morgan says that building relationships with community groups was the top priority for her when she joined the Luke Center shortly after its formation. She reached out to nonprofits across the state and made the center's philosophy clear: We don't want giving at Punahou to be about Punahou, we want it to be about giving. Tell us what you need, and we'll figure out how we can make it happen. A charity that needs school supplies shouldn't be getting donations of canned beans. "If you really want to be of service, you shouldn't be a burden to those you're trying to help," she says.

Before Punahou founded the Luke Center, she notes, students and faculty were doing many different service projects, but had no central point of coordination. Nonprofits had multiple contacts at the school, rather than one contact to whom they could communicate their needs. When launching a project, teachers often had to start from scratch, building a relationship with a group, before they could even begin to plan what they'd ask students to do. Since the launch of the Luke Center, the number of volunteer opportunities at Punahou has increased, and those experiences offer greater depth. Students are going beyond their initial gift of time, donations, or both, and forming strong ties with nonprofits and the people they serve.

Some of those students have become Luke Leaders, middle-school and Academy students who volunteer with the center for at least one year to assist with public service initiatives. Luke Leaders have donated their time to community literacy programs, homeless shelters, and sustainability organizations. They have also sought to bolster service learning on campus: Some assist other students in finding the right opportunity; others volunteer alongside chaplains to present service learning themes. Since the center's inception, it has worked with nearly 400 Luke Leaders.

Alayna Kobayashi '14 was one of those leaders. She started working with the Luke Center

With a sophisticated, modern aesthetic responsive
to local conditions of climate and topography, Vladimir
Ossipoff designed two complexes on campus—the
Mary Persis Winne Elementary Units (1955) with the
Julia Ing Learning Center (1990); and the Robert Shipman
Thurston Jr. Memorial Chapel (1966). He also designed
the flagstone plaza at the entrance to the H. Gaylord
Dillingham Tennis Courts (1949).

At the dedication of Thurston Chapel, Ossipoff
described his goals for integrating all aspects of this
striking site, "To integrate the chapel with the site
and the lily pond, which is so much a part of Punahou's
lore, we lowered the chapel's floor below the court to
bring it physically closer to the pond and, to integrate
it even further, a portion of the pond itself has been
incorporated within the chapel walls...I hope that
a sense of belonging has been achieved."

75

Vertical bands of stained glass designed by Erica Karawina create a dazzling spectrum of refracted light in the dark sanctuary. Rows of pews designed by Ossipoff reveal the gentle slope of the floor downward toward the altar situated at the level of the spring.

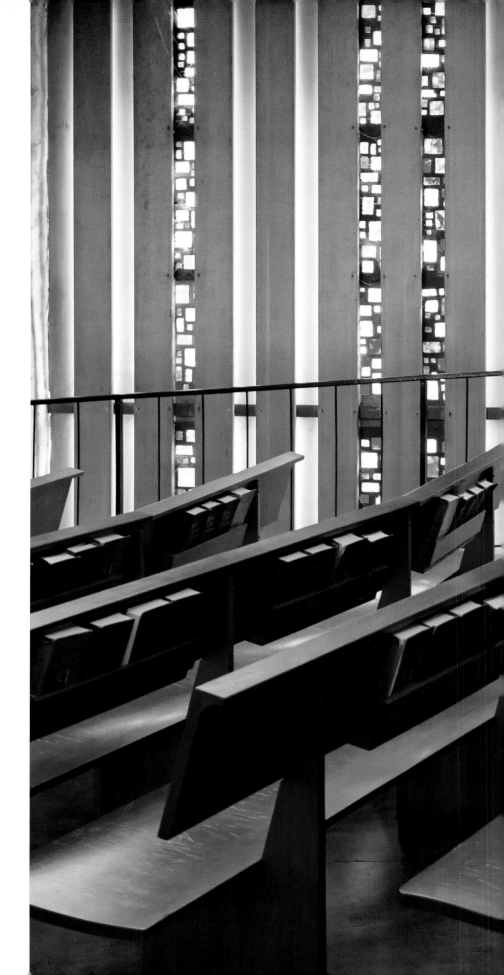

in sixth grade, and was among the group of students teaching hydroponics to children at Next Step in Kakaʻako. When I met her at the shelter, she told me simply, "My high-school experience in public service has culminated with this project." Kobayashi has participated in public service work throughout her time at Punahou, which she entered in kindergarten. But Next Step was special: With the help of her group, she was able to transform an idea into reality. The students contacted the homeless shelter, set up a schedule of visits, developed a curriculum, gathered supplies, and assessed their progress. They made the project happen, from start to finish. At Punahou, she says, she's learned the importance of getting to know the world around you and the problems people face. She's also learned the importance of "taking that personal knowledge to help the community, to be able to give back."

The Luke Center celebrated its tenth anniversary in 2014, and now Morgan is looking ahead to envision how the program can continue to grow—and give more students experiences like Kobayashi's. Luke Leaders volunteer as part of an extracurricular program, but Morgan is interested in offering credit courses and in bringing alumni back to campus to act as mentors. Morgan also wants to give more students—whether they're leaders or not—the opportunity to participate in in-depth public volunteering off campus. The majority of service projects still primarily happen on campus, but it's vital that students work more often alongside those they're seeking to help, she says: "So it's not us and them. It's not me doing for you, but you and me doing something together, knowing each other, understanding each other."

Punahou intentionally built the Luke Center adjacent to Kapunahou and Thurston Memorial Chapel. Together, the three structures make up the heart of the campus—a gathering place where Junior School and Academy students intermingle. On sunny afternoons, students congregate in the area for quiet lunches or conversations. Scott says his challenge to Morgan and to the chaplains is to "activate that whole chapel area"—to create a hub of activity, attach rigor to public service projects, coordinate them more effectively, and convene community conversations about service and need. The Luke Center's proximity to the chapel also underscores the strong connection between the two: Service projects bring into focus the chapel's messages about humanity and humility, about caring for friends and strangers, about paying attention to your own backyard and someone else's, about growth and understanding.

To put it another way, at the Luke Center, students turn the chaplains' big messages into concrete action. Nondenominational themes for students serve as a backdrop for public service work, says Chaplain Joshua Hayashi, and for exploring significant questions about goodness,

Sophie Judd

THE OAHUAN

PUBLISHED BY THE
SENIOR CLASS
PUNAHOU SCHOOL
1929

HONOLULU, HAWAII

values, and ethics. For the theme of the *gift*, for example, chaplains pressed students to ask themselves, how can you think about yourself as a gift? What gifts do you have to share?

Students are exposed to service learning themes throughout the school year, starting on the first day of every school year at the annual convocation, the only time Punahou addresses all its students at once. Regular chapel services, convened by grade level, also integrate those themes. "We have an opportunity to have quite the conversation with the entire campus," says Chaplain Lauren Buck Medeiros. "We're physiologically and psychologically connected to service. And for faith, any kind of faith, talking about it is one thing, but putting it into action is really what's important. With these service themes, we have an opportunity to introduce them or to inspire in this space, and then have actual action items that can come from it."

Not just a summer program ∼

Up until the sixth grade, Yuna Martin was better known at school for the fights she got into than for her academic record. She had so-so grades and a tough family life; she didn't do any thinking about high school, much less college. But at the close of her fifth-grade year, in 2005, she had an opportunity. Her elementary-school principal asked her if she wanted to attend summer school at Punahou as part of a new program called Partnerships in Unlimited Educational Opportunities (PUEO). Martin figured it wouldn't hurt to try, so she joined the inaugural cohort of 40 students from 14 public schools admitted into the program.

Over the last decade, PUEO has garnered national attention for its innovative approach to helping middle-of-the-road students from low-income backgrounds prepare for—and imagine themselves in—college. Martin, who is now studying psychology at the University of Hawai'i, says that stepping onto the Punahou campus for the first time was like being sent off to Hogwarts, the witchcraft and wizardry school in the Harry Potter series, where everything seemed possible and kids who were struggling in the outside world started to see themselves as special in this new place. Suddenly, she identified herself as a scholar—someone who could actually achieve in school. She started to believe in herself and to consider her future. While she was growing up, Martin says, "We were on welfare. I didn't think of college as something I could afford. I didn't think I had the ability to achieve that high." But at PUEO, college was the expectation. That was the starting point. "I don't know where I would be without PUEO," she adds. "It probably wouldn't be in college."

PUEO traces its roots back to 2000, when Carl Ackerman, now PUEO's program director, took a one-year sabbatical to work with the Hawai'i Department of Education. He was there to help bolster service learning opportunities for students, but also to make connections with department personnel, who could offer insight into what a successful program for public-school students at Punahou might look like. After Ackerman returned to Punahou, he led a small team charged with researching public programs at private schools in the continental United States and drafting a proposal for something similar at Punahou. When Punahou gave Ackerman the green light to proceed with launching PUEO, it also gave him a hefty task: Find funding, find students, make it work.

And that's just what PUEO did. By the end of its first year, Punahou knew it had something: PUEO students were engaged and interested in what they were learning; after a single summer, some had turned around academically. Those early results helped PUEO make its funding case and begin to build a sustainable program. In its first five years, PUEO garnered initial funding from major donors including the Harold K. L. Castle Foundation, The Harry and Jeanette Weinberg Foundation, and Unbound Philanthropy.

PUEO's genius may lie in its simplicity. Principals or teachers select academically average, low-income public-school sixth graders for entrance into the program. For seven years, the scholars attend Punahou's summer school. Along with taking classes in marine biology or robotics or Hawaiian history, they visit colleges, attend academic counseling sessions, and get assistance in filling out applications for colleges, scholarships, and financial aid. They have support and guidance, some of it from their peers. Every year, PUEO employs Punahou graduates and other college students as mentors. Now, some PUEO graduates—including Yuna Martin—are mentors.

Thanks to major gifts from the Clarence T. C. Ching Foundation, the program will continue through the next decade to serve close to 300 students each year, an average of 40 in each cohort from sixth to twelfth grade. As of 2014, all of PUEO's 119 alumni had graduated from high school, and 85 percent were enrolled in college. According to Kylee Mar, PUEO's assistant director, the magic that happens in the program isn't all that mysterious. Punahou is doing for PUEO kids what it does for its own students: It's giving them tough standards to meet, offering them imaginative, high-quality instruction, and putting them in an environment where they feel that anything is possible.

When PUEO students enter the program that first summer, they might just be realizing where they stand academically and what their family's socioeconomic status means for their

chances in school and in life. "The culture they come from at home is not one of a lot of hope about college," Mar says. "We try to shift that culture to show them there are other opportunities. It's a culture of college that provides them with the ability to see there are more doors to their future. We actually have them choose what that door looks like. It's this sense of empowerment—that they can do it."

Though the Clarence T. C. Ching PUEO program takes place during the summer, President Jim Scott doesn't see it as disconnected or supplemental to the work Punahou is doing every day. Rather, it is central to Punahou's mission as a school dedicated to giving back, and to ensuring that the education happening on Punahou's campus is not reserved only for those who can afford it. PUEO, says Scott, is one way the school is living up to the charge it gives its students: that they have a duty to their community and an obligation to their neighbors. Punahou is internationally acclaimed for its record of preparing young people for college, and so it made "intuitive sense," Scott says, "to do what we do well" in a public program.

Now communities across the state have PUEO students. Their parents can say their children have gone to Punahou, and their pride in that has also helped break down persistent and negative notions of Punahou as an elite school for the wealthy, with sheltered, out-of-touch students. Mar, the assistant director, adds that PUEO has given Punahou the opportunity to be a part of the "village"—helping to raise kids who need some extra assistance—and has offered Punahou students the chance to interact and work with peers who see the world differently. "We've seen our scholars go through deaths of parents, marriages, divorces, children themselves having children, everything," she says. "PUEO is the safety net. We are the place where some of them will get their only meal of the day in summer. We are the people they call when they're worried they're going to flunk out of high school."

Martin, who graduated from PUEO in 2012, found a second family in the program—people who were interested in her success and could give her tools to achieve her goals. It's why she has committed to returning to the program every summer as a college mentor. She wants other kids to have what she had, to know they belong. "PUEO, it's not just a summer program," she tells me. "Kids who feel they don't belong or don't see how great they can be, they enter PUEO and see these doors open, they see that they can do anything." PUEO is why when people say that Punahou and its students are out of touch, Martin urges them to take a second look. Don't judge so quickly, she tells them, because "look at what Punahou did for me."

I still remember that ethics class ⌒

No tour of Punahou's campus is complete without a visit to Kapunahou, the freshwater spring known on campus as the Lily Pond. There, visitors see a plaque commemorating the "original gift"—the gift of land from Hawaiian aliʻi to Punahou's missionary founders. The occasion of an anniversary is an opportunity to celebrate beginnings and mark progress. It's also a chance to identify shortcomings and address gaps. As Punahou celebrates its 175th anniversary, its teachers, administrators, students, and alumni are thinking back on the promise of the school— on its founding; on its infancy and adolescence; and on how it has gained stature and become a pillar of educational excellence in Hawaiʻi and nationally. Many of them are also looking to the future. For a school that has made a significant and sustained commitment to public service—that identifies itself as a private school with a public purpose—that future means building on its work to instill children with a sense of obligation, of duty, and of understanding about the world beyond Punahou's walls. In that self-examination, the school must ask: How do we shape new educational opportunities so that learning about and doing public service resonates with children and prompts them to individual action?

That's no easy task—what moves one student might not move another. "You never know what they're going to experience or get that will actually make a difference in their lives and then make a difference to their communities as well," says Medeiros, the elementary-school chaplain. She points to a back-to-school speech Punahou alumnus President Barack Obama made in 2011 at a high school in Washington, DC. In it, he pointed to the transformative nature of an ethics class he took at Punahou in eighth grade. "I still remember that ethics class, all these years later," Obama said. "I remember the way it made me think. I remember being asked questions like: What matters in life? Or, what does it mean to treat other people with dignity and respect? What does it mean to live in a diverse nation, where not everybody looks like you do, or thinks like you do, or comes from the same neighborhood as you do? . . . I didn't always know the right answers, but those discussions and that process of discovery—those things have lasted."

Other alumni who have sought out careers in public service recall their own transformative experiences at Punahou. For Colin Kippen '67, who served as coordinator on homelessness under Gov. Neil Abercrombie, it was hearing civil rights activists speak at chapel. "I can remember hanging on every word," Kippen says. "'You can do something.' That was a big part of the message." For Terry George '76, president and chief executive officer of the Harold K. L. Castle Foundation, it was reading the then-controversial book *The Limits to Growth* in class and talking about environmental sustainability with his peers. "There were opportunities for deep inquiry on where we're headed as a planet," George notes.

But even as alumni point to their own experiences at Punahou, and applaud the work that has brought into sharper focus the notion of Punahou as a school with a public purpose, they acknowledge that more work lies ahead. A natural next step for Punahou, says George, is helping students begin to explore how to actually tackle some of the problems they're learning about in public service projects. Students should be grappling with big questions that affect both the globe and their own backyards. "We need to help students learn who they are and what values shape Hawai'i. We need to let them know they are change agents right now," he says. "They don't have to wait to be adults before they can start making Hawai'i a better place."

Back at the Next Step Shelter, the Punahou students are packing up and saying their good-byes. Alayna Kobayashi's mom is waiting in the parking lot, smiling as she watches her daughter offer a few last-minute instructions to children. Danette Kobayashi, who teaches at Punahou, says she has seen the school's dedication to public service change her daughter—and her own classroom. It was with some trepidation that Kobayashi took a position at Punahou after teaching at Makaha Elementary School. She knew what impact she was having on kids in Mākaha, but when she looked at her students at Punahou, she wasn't sure if they really needed her. They would do fine without her, she thought.

But Kobayashi came to recognize that her role at Punahou was to help kids who have so much—a high-quality education, a supportive community, limitless opportunity—to "embrace a culture of service." The same qualities she wanted to see in her daughter, which her daughter was demonstrating through service learning and giving, were the ones she wanted to instill in her students. "I realized my goal is to help these future leaders develop depth and compassion and empathy," she concludes. Punahou shares that goal.

In 1853, a smallpox epidemic struck Honolulu with devastating effects on the Native Hawaiian population, who had no immunity to the contagious and often fatal disease. Punahou suspended classes during the epidemic and teacher William Harrison Rice and his wife, Mary Sophia, devoted themselves to caring for the afflicted. A makeshift hospital was erected near the intersection of the current Wilder and Alexander Streets.

On Maui, Dr. Baldwin instituted quarantine procedures to halt the spread of the disease. He also traveled across the island and to Molokaʻi and Lānaʻi to vaccinate as many people as he could. "I shall go over to Lanai, meet all the people (600)— examine their arms and vaccinate all who need it," he wrote in an 1853 letter to his son. Baldwin's tireless efforts to protect residents on Maui, Molokaʻi, and Lānaʻi from the ravages of the disease saved innumerable lives. Fifteen thousand people died of smallpox in Honolulu, but only two hundred succumbed to the disease on Maui.

Rev. Dwight Baldwin, pastor and physician, and Charlotte Fowler Baldwin, arrived in Hawaiʻi in 1831. After an initial posting in Waimea on Hawaiʻi Island, the couple was assigned to Lahaina, Maui, then the capital of the Hawaiian Kingdom. There Rev. Baldwin took charge of Waineʻe Church, the great stone church built under the leadership of Hoapili and dedicated in 1832. Both Hoapili and his daughter Liliha are buried in the adjoining cemetery.

Serving the large Native Hawaiian community there, he was highly regarded for his dedication and caring disposition. Dr. Baldwin ran a dispensary out of the family home, and Mrs. Baldwin held classes on the lānai, instructing women in various school subjects, sewing, and knitting. In addition to spiritual and physical ministering, Dr. Baldwin worked to advance the cause of education, including serving as a founding trustee of Punahou School.

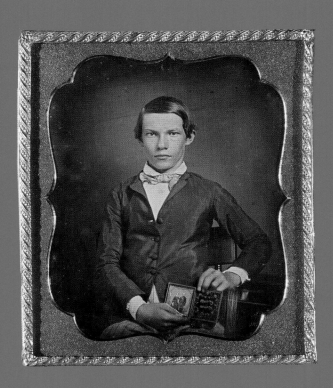

Charles Fowler Baldwin (1847–48) was the fourth of Dwight and Charlotte Baldwin's eight children. Dr. Baldwin refers to this daguerreotype in a letter to his daughter, Abigail, dated January 1854, "Charles, when taken, held open in his hands the picture of you and Dwight, and there you will see your own figures." Abigail (1844–49) and her brother, David Dwight (1844–51), were both attending school in New England when the daguerreotype of their younger brother was delivered to her.

Julia Kealoha was a beloved caregiver to the Baldwin family for forty years, caring especially for Charlotte Baldwin, who often was unwell. Kealoha's affection for the Baldwin children is evident in numerous letters that Dr. Baldwin wrote them, in which he conveys Kealoha's greetings of love. She holds a daguerreotype of the two eldest children, David Dwight and Abigail. Kealoha was born in Hāmākua, Hawai'i, in 1798 and witnessed the social upheavals that transformed Hawai'i in the nineteenth century.

Samuel P. King, US Naval Intelligence officer, c. 1944. Sam credits his learning of Japanese vocabulary and katakana as a child for positively affecting his application to the Navy's Japanese Language School in 1943.

While students at Central Grammar School near downtown Honolulu, Sam and his sister Charlotte would wait after school for their father to finish work before he picked them up for the ride home. Several times a week, during this wait time, Sam attended Hongwanji Mission Academy's Japanese language school. When his active duty ended in 1946, Sam continued on in the US Naval Reserve until 1967.

SAMUEL P. KING 1933

BY RANDALL ROTH

Samuel Pailthorpe King '33 served Hawai'i for fifty years as the state's best-known state and federal court judge. Sam was known for his wit, wisdom, and predictable fairness while on the bench, but his life outside the courtroom also had a profound impact on his generation and those that followed.

Though Sam was born in China, where his father, Samuel Wilder King, served as the captain of a US Navy gunboat, he had deep roots in Hawai'i. He was a descendant of ali'i on both sides of the family tree. On his father's side, haole ancestor Oliver Holmes arrived in the islands in 1793, advised Kamehameha I, and later became governor of O'ahu. Holmes married Mahi, daughter of Kalaniho'oulumokuikekai, an O'ahu ali'i. Sam's mother, Pauline Nawahineokala'i Evans, had ali'i roots on Maui; her great-grandfather was named Kaniau.

Sam lost an eye in an accident at home when he was six years old, but he never let that loss define or discourage him. Years later, when he captained Punahou's rifle team, he would sometimes say that he had the unfair advantage of not having to close one eye while aiming at the target.

Early on Sam showed a talent for languages and for expressing himself. He took French lessons to gain entry to Punahou for high school, and learned

Japanese at the insistence of his father. Winning the Damon Speech Contest gave him the confidence to enter the National Oratorical Contest in 1933, and then travel to Europe with the other winning finalists. He shared his adventures abroad in a *Honolulu Star-Bulletin* column called "To Europe with Sam King."

After earning his law degree at Yale Law School, Sam worked his way back home in 1940 on a freighter, spending six hours a day steering the vessel and the rest of his time studying for the bar exam. While waiting for his results, he taught math at Punahou.

Sam joined the Office of Naval Intelligence shortly after the bombing of Pearl Harbor, and his service included translating for Navy brass as they toured the rubble in Hiroshima, and for Allied forces as they searched for mines in Tokyo Bay. Talking about it years later, Sam made this work sound like just another day at the office: "Translating mine charts wasn't too hard. I just had to identify the area, and then the distance and the speed. It was all in Japanese, but it was very simple Japanese."

Sam cared about everybody, and he acted on his sense of compassion. Following the war, he declined invitations from established law firms so that he could run his own practice. When local leftists faced charges in the late 1940s for "un-American" activities, Sam called the accusations a witch hunt and represented those individuals without charge. Later, as a judge, Sam would visit convicts he had sentenced to federal penitentiaries on the continental United States, to make sure the facilities were treating them properly.

Also as a judge, he made landmark decisions:

under their homes; and he rejected evidence acquired by using a high-powered telescope to peer into a suspect's home.

But Sam never took himself, or anyone else, too seriously. He was well known for referring to the members of the US Supreme Court as "the guys in the black muʻumuʻus."

In 1997, Sam spearheaded the writing of the "Broken Trust" manifesto, which leveled charges of corruption against the politically powerful Bishop Estate trustees and the Supreme Court justices who had appointed them. The resulting controversy saw the trustees forced from office and the justices removed from the trustee selection process. None of it would have happened without the intervention of Sam King, who was 83 years old at the time.

In 2006, Sam and I told this story in a best-selling book, *Broken Trust*, that garnered critical praise internationally and earned "Book of the Year" honors in 2007 from the Hawaii Book Publishers Association. At his suggestion, we gave all the royalties to early education charities in Hawaiʻi.

Sam kept working until shortly before his death at age 94. When he died on December 7, 2010, Hawaiʻi lost one of its greatest minds and finest sons—and I lost one of my best friends.

At the King family home in Halekou, Kāneʻohe, 1945:

(front row) Samuel Wilder King, Pauline Nawahineokalaʻi King '42, Pauline Nawahineokalaʻi Evans King;

(middle row) Evans Palikū King '41, Charlotte King '32 McAndrews, Anne Grilk King;

(back row) Davis Mauliola King '40, James McAndrews, Samuel Pailthorpe King '33.

He allowed an environmental lawsuit in the name of a threatened native bird species to proceed; he declared unconstitutional the involuntary commitment of the mentally ill who pose no threat to themselves or to others; he upheld legislation making it possible for leaseholders to buy the land

THE REPPUN FAMILY

BY CATHERINE MARIKO BLACK '94

In 1919, against the turbulent backdrop of the Russian Revolution and civil war, Dr. Carl Reppun bundled his wife, Emily, and their two young boys, Frederick and Eric, into a single-horse carriage and rode a thousand miles across the Siberian steppes. In Omsk, the family intersected with the American Expeditionary Forces, including the American Red Cross; once the Red Cross discovered that Carl was an educated physician who spoke four languages, they enlisted him to treat the wounded from all sides of the conflict.

Born on the French Riviera, raised in Latvia, and married to a Welsh governess, Carl never imagined he would live out his days on a tiny archipelago in the middle of the Pacific. But in 1920—with the help of Riley Allen, a longtime *Honolulu Star-Bulletin* editor and the head of the American Red Cross in Siberia at the time—the Reppuns obtained passage on the last ship to carry American personnel out of Russia, embarking from Vladivostok. They disembarked in Honolulu.

The high intellectual standards they brought with them would profoundly influence the family they raised. Carl served as a government physician and plantation doctor for the McNeill & Libby Pineapple operation in Kahaluʻu, where the family

opposite
Paul Reppun and his granddaughter
Makakailenuiaola Diane Dickson,
Waiāhole Valley, c. 1996

lived before moving to Mānoa. All three sons enrolled at Punahou School (Arthur was born shortly after the family arrived in Honolulu). After graduating from Harvard University, Frederick '32 followed his father into a family practice. Eric '34

was named Hawaiʻi's first president of the Board of Commissioners of Agriculture and Forestry, and Arthur '39 became an international manager for Pan American Airways.

After spending ten years as a country doctor on Lānaʻi and Molokaʻi, Frederick purchased three acres of land across the street from his parents' old bungalow in Kahaluʻu. In the shade of several enormous monkeypod trees, he built the house in which he and his wife, Jean, would raise their seven children. Like him, they would grow up roaming the lush Windward coast at a time when creeping urban development and militarization were beginning to disrupt its rural rhythm. Like him, they all entered Punahou in the seventh grade but received a significant dose of additional instruction at home. The dinner table was the setting for many lively intellectual and political debates, often sparked by an article that Frederick read aloud. Books held an important place in the household.

Frederick and Jean were staunch community activists, and their children inherited their fearlessness and tenacity: Charlie '65 and Paul '68 are taro farmers whose names are synonymous with efforts to preserve Hawaiʻi's water and food sovereignty; John '70 is the executive director of the KEY Project, one of the most respected community organiza-

The Reppuns at the family home in Kahaluʻu, c. 1978—(clockwise from front center) matriarch Jean, John ʼ70, Tom ʼ67, Charlie ʼ65, David ʼ72, patriarch Fred ʼ32, Paul ʼ68, Josh ʼ76, and Martha ʼ63.

opposite
Tai Crouch, co-director of Gates Science Center, directs imu activities in the Winne Unit's Hawaiian garden in preparation for Third-Grade Lūʻau.

tions on the Windward side; Josh ʼ76 is an innovative teacher who helped found one of Hawaiʻi's first sustainability-based charter schools; Tom ʼ67 is a pathologist; David ʼ72 is also a farmer; and eldest sister Martha ʼ63 is the keeper of the family lore. Wherever the Reppuns pass, they leave a trail of social and environmental activism, progressive education, and a branching family tree that currently includes 19 graduates of Punahou School.

The family's iconoclastic combination of education, leadership, and service is evident in a visit to Charlie and Paul's farm deep in Waiāhole Valley. Equal parts learning laboratory and political statement, its off-the-grid utopia mingles elements of a bucolic rural past with a fierce optimism about alternative futures.

Charlie and Paul say they began farming taro in the 1970s to "get out of the system," but it wasn't long before their talent for questioning that system got the better of them. Who really benefited from urban development? Why was water being diverted from Windward streams? Their insistence helped avert a major real estate development in Waiāhole and Waikāne valleys and contributed to the Supreme Court of Hawaiʻi's reaffirmation of the doctrine of water as a public trust resource.

"You can't run away from information when you know what's going on," says Paul, who grad- uated from Harvard like his father, but maintains that he learned more from farming than from school. That may be why he and Charlie regularly welcome school groups to the farm, where children can plunge knee-deep in the loʻi and learn about energy, ecology, and food production —twenty-first-century challenges that the brothers tackle with passion and urgency.

"I've always thought that a good education teaches you how to ask good questions," reflects Charlie. "So what do we want to be teaching kids? Is it simply to make a good living? Or is it to go out and change the world?"

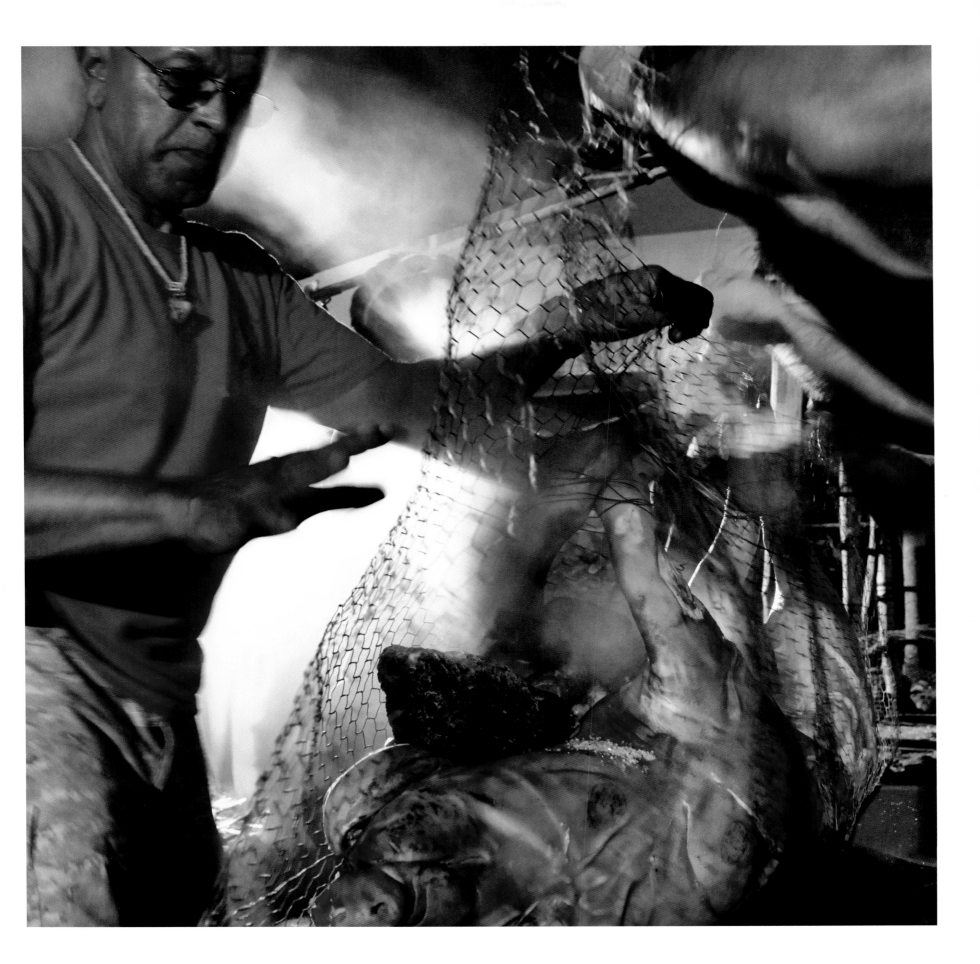

Each March, the Mary Persis Winne Elementary Units come alive with the sights, sounds, and smells of Third-Grade Lūʻau. The event is the highlight of the students' yearlong study of Hawaiian culture, which builds upon the concept of the ahupuaʻa and the Hawaiian values of aloha, laulima, and mālama ʻāina introduced in the earlier grades. The children grow ʻuala, kalo, and wauke, weave their own lauhala headbands and placemats, and learn the oli and mele of Kapunahou.

Principal Mary Winne, for whom the Winne Units are named, was a strong proponent of teaching Hawaiian culture. In 1928–29, she invited her friend, Keahi Luahine, to instruct fifth graders in kapa making. The renowned hula practitioner, whose hānai daughter was ʻIolani Luahine, showed the students "how to strip the bark from our own wauke plants" and "how to prepare it for beating," Winne wrote in her annual report.

By 1931, the knowledgeable and patient Mary Kawena Pukui was conducting weekly classes for grades two to six. Along with recounting Hawaiian stories, proverbs, and riddles, Pukui taught the students to play the ipu, kālaʻau, pūʻili, and ʻiliʻili.

Students today develop an understanding of Hawaiian culture through courses that include an after-school Hawaiian language immersion program, traveling to Hawaiʻi Island to study volcanoes in fifth grade, and five levels of Hawaiian language.

Castle Hall was home to Punahou's fifth- and sixth-grade classes before the opening of Case Middle School in 2005. Today Castle is home to fourth- and fifth-grade classes, Junior School administration, and art and music studios for the elementary grades.

A SCHOOL OF THE ISLANDS

JAMES KOSHIBA '91

Case Middle School provides a learning environment tailored to the developmental needs of young adolescents. Steve '76 and Jean Case and the Case family donated funds toward the construction of the nine-building complex, named in honor of Daniel H. '42 and Carol Case.

The Case Middle School complex for sixth, seventh, and eighth grades was designed by architect John Hara '57 as nine separate buildings on four acres of land. Each floor of adjacent classrooms, designed to foster a sense of community among students and staff, supports a team of English, math, science, and social studies teachers who collaborate to integrate studies.

The complex was envisioned to fit neatly within the existing campus, respectful of Punahou's architectural landmarks. Situated on a steep slope, Case Middle School offers dramatic views of the city and ocean that are especially striking given the village-like nature of both the middle school complex and the overall campus. Case Middle School was named "Greenest School in America" in 2006 and was the first major certified "green" project in Hawai'i.

Twenty-five years ago in the book *Punahou: The History and Promise of a School of the Islands*, Mindy Pennybacker '70 contributed the thought-provoking essay "The Haole Rich Kid's School: An Update." The essay tackled, in incisive fashion, the perception and reality behind Punahou's reputation as an elite—and elitist—institution. Through interviews with Punahou trustees, alumni, and administrators, as well as public school students and educators, Pennybacker portrayed a school that by 1991 had taken "promising steps" toward increasing diversity and changing its image. She found a student body that was no longer predominantly Caucasian, and a Punahou that had strengthened relationships with public schools and opened some of its facilities to the community. Yet she also found that many still perceived it as a bastion of privilege—as a public high school student put it, "It's just, like, a rich kids' school now."

"Promising steps are not great strides," Pennybacker surmised, adding, "If Punahou means to represent and to serve the community as a whole . . . the socioeconomic gates of the school must be *thrown* open; they will not open of their own accord." She concluded with her hope that "school leaders will have the courage to make . . . hard choices, to forgo campus improvements, say, in favor of a new outreach and financial aid program, or to turn down more alumni children and missionary descendants, if need be, to achieve a fair student mix before Punahou turns two hundred."

Jim Scott read Pennybacker's essay shortly before he interviewed for the position of Punahou School president. "It was one of the things that inspired me to pursue the job," he says. To Scott, the fact that Punahou had published such an essay signaled the courage Pennybacker had called for—a willingness to tackle sensitive topics, to hold up the mirror and ask hard questions.

Soon after the school hired him, Scott tested the ground that Pennybacker had staked out. In one of his first addresses as president, he shared his own provocative vision of Punahou's contribution to the community and its commitment to student financial aid. His statements reached beyond racial diversity, setting the school's sights on increased socioeconomic diversity, and he highlighted a new trustee-approved budget, which increased financial aid by 20 percent.

On the heels of those statements, he advanced his own tough questions: "Can we sustain such a commitment?" "Is Punahou ready and willing to accommodate more economic diversity within its student body?" And finally, "To whom should financial aid be distributed and why?"

This last question of "who and why" would present Punahou's greatest challenge and opportunity, echoing across a quarter century of work undertaken to increase access and diversity. Scott's question would present new horizons in admissions and programming that the school had never before considered. It would also pose new problems to solve, for Punahou had yet to tap its promise as an institution born of the melting pot of Hawaiʻi.

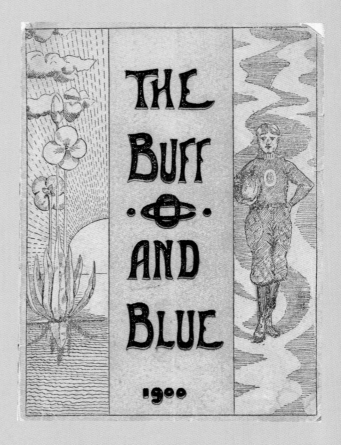

Scott's address in 1994 did not immediately convince everyone at Punahou that the school should elevate financial aid to a top priority. In the 1980s and early 1990s, administrators and trustees had identified an urgent need to strengthen Punahou's bottom line. To some, a move to increase aid seemed counterproductive—a "noble, but expensive" endeavor, as the school's annual report noted later that year. Others worried that increasing financial aid would require tuition increases, having the net effect of making Punahou less accessible. Conversation on these topics was on-going as administrators and trustees set to work on addressing the question of whether Punahou could sustain its commitment to financial aid.

In 1994, the primary sources of funding for financial aid at Punahou consisted of net income from Carnival and endowed scholarships. The amount available for aid fluctuated from year to year depending on the Carnival weekend's weather and the number of donors seeking to establish a scholarship fund. Scott's vision would require new sources of funding to stabilize and expand the amounts available for financial aid each year.

Punahou began with internal commitments to tuition assistance for applicants exhibiting "high promise, but limited economic opportunity." The school expanded the Trustee Scholars Program, with funds for new students entering Punahou in grades six to eight. Punahou also diversified its endowment portfolio, hired a professional investment advisor, and took steps to ensure that the returns could support the new initiatives.

To make sure that increased aid would not detract from other budget priorities, the president, board, and administrative staff launched a concerted effort to expand the asset base for financial assistance. Fund-raising for financial aid was unfamiliar territory. Donors are accustomed to giving for things that are visible—buildings, lab equipment, library carrels. They're less likely to give to programs, since these funds pay for intangible, recurring expenses such as staff, instruction, and operations. Even the most impactful instructional program may never draw wide recognition unless the institution publicizes it.

Aware of these obstacles, Punahou made a special effort to build relationships with donors who might give specifically toward financial aid. The school worked to connect with a new generation of alumni, many of whom had made their wealth on the continent and returned to Hawaiʻi because they wanted their children to benefit from both a Punahou education and the cultural diversity of the islands. Increasing financial aid—and through it the socioeconomic diversity of Punahou's student body—might offer compelling benefits to these alumni and their children.

For the next two decades, the amounts raised and allocated for financial aid grew, quadrupling between 1994 and 2014. The number of students admitted on financial aid grew as well, from 350 students in the early 1990s to more than 560 by 2014. Today, about one in seven students enrolled at Punahou receives direct tuition assistance, based on demonstrated financial need determined by a review of family income and assets. This ratio does not account for the tuition remissions offered to children of faculty and staff; nor does it take into account the fact that the school subsidizes every student, since tuition covers only about 80 percent of the cost of a Punahou education.

The school's commitment to increased aid faced a test when the financial crisis of 2008 unfolded. The endowments of many independent schools shrank overnight, as did the incomes of tuition-paying families. Those schools with reserves dipped into them; others cut the budgets of various departments, including financial aid. At Punahou, in contrast, the trustees decided to *increase* tuition assistance, allocating additional funds to support enrolled families whose financial circumstances had changed as a result of the recession. The move helped Punahou sustain a strong admissions profile throughout the economic downturn.

Heroic and largely untouted victories lie behind the growth in financial aid—the challenging work of building new relationships with alumni, the generosity and creativity of donors and trustees, savvy financial strategy and disciplined cost controls, and the persistent quest to align mission, message, and means. Turning that "noble, but expensive" vision into an established initiative during decades that saw the worst economy since the Great Depression was in itself an accomplishment to celebrate. And yet Punahou's vision for increasing access and diversity proved to be even more complicated and more ambitious than that.

In the years since World War II, Punahou students have come primarily from middle- and upper-income suburban neighborhoods of Oʻahu, and from families in which at least one adult attended college. Those entering Punahou in middle or high school have often arrived from other private schools.

As Punahou expanded financial aid, it admitted more students from households of modest financial means, from rural communities, and from families with no college (or college prep) experience. Though they still comprised just a fraction of annual admissions, the growing number of such students added urgency to another question the president had raised in 1994—was Punahou ready to accommodate greater economic diversity?

One summer in the early 2000s, Punahou admitted an outstanding young man into the ninth grade. The transcript from his public middle school consisted of straight A's. Past instructors submitted effusive recommendation letters. His peers had elected him class president and May Day king. Everything indicated his ability to succeed socially and academically at Punahou. The school admitted him on financial aid, based upon his family's demonstrated need.

Three weeks into Punahou's new school year, this young man had already missed several days of school. Calls to his home went unreturned. Eventually, an Academy dean paid a personal visit to the address listed in the student's file. He found a one-room apartment that the boy shared with seven siblings, his mother, and his older sister's young children.

The visit revealed that the boy had, in fact, set out for school each day, riding his bicycle to Punahou and circling the campus. On some days he mustered the nerve to enter. On other days he returned home. What kept him away were fears that he would not fit in. Did anyone else at Punahou balance a job, babysitting, and homework, for instance? Was anyone else striving to be the first in their family to graduate from high school? With encouragement from adults and peers, this student eventually made it to class, and he thrived at Punahou. In response to his experience, the school began to examine the need to provide transitional assistance for students arriving via less traveled and less privileged paths.

In 2004, the school launched the Bridge Program to provide academic and social support to students entering ninth grade from schools and communities with little knowledge of Punahou or academic settings like it. Each year, Bridge engages a cohort of fifteen to twenty freshmen. The summer before they start at Punahou, they work closely with four faculty members to prepare academically for the coming school year and to become familiar with campus conventions. A cohort stays together through the entire ninth grade, meeting daily for group study hall, with ongoing support from faculty mentors.

Over the years, Bridge has helped expose gaps between Punahou's standard assumptions about students and the varied realities these new students bring to campus. Occasionally the distinctions are striking. "We'd ask some students to turn on the computer, and they'd ask, 'Where's the button?'" recalls Lynn Kimura '81 Kunishige, Bridge Program coordinator. At Punahou, student-teacher meetings during office hours are a regular occurrence. Some incoming students had never met alone with a teacher, and saw such meetings as a sign of weakness

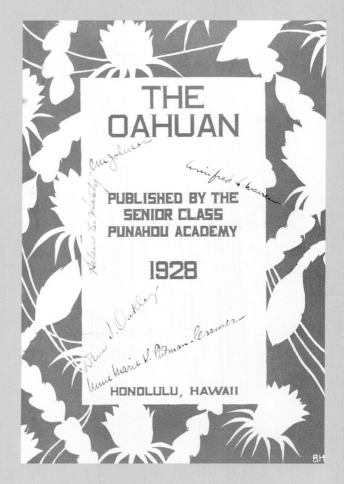

or failure. Homework assignments at Punahou often required Web-based research, and some of these students didn't have computers or Internet access at home.

Bridge evolved to meet a range of needs. It began offering information and support to families about school activities, the use of technology at Punahou, and traditions such as volunteering at at Carnival. Faculty mentors began interacting regularly with family, parents, and students on a variety of topics, including playing sports, selecting extracurriculars, and preparing for college applications. "The point is for every student to know that every single day there are faculty members thinking about their success," says James Kakos, an Academy dean who heads the Bridge Program.

Kakos and Kunishige are rightly proud of the students they've mentored over the years. Some have gone on to Stanford, Yale, and other elite universities; others have launched careers in finance, academia, or the arts. At the time of this writing, one graduate had just become a practicing veterinarian. But Bridge does more than equip new students for Punahou; it has also equipped the school to serve a more diverse student body—identifying barriers to student success that stemmed from Punahou's own assumptions about wealth and culture rather than from students' talent or work ethic.

Beyond the Bridge Program, Punahou has also taken a proactive approach, retooling overall campus practices to reflect a more socially and economically diverse student and parent body. The school has adjusted the timing of some meetings and events to make them accessible to working parents with long commutes. It has reimagined junior prom as a more casual function without the tuxedoes, limousines, and other trappings that can strain family budgets.

Still, acting as diversity pioneers can be hard on students. In a recent study of the Bridge Program, one student reported, "I don't feel like people hold me accountable . . . because 'Oh, she's just a Bridge kid.' I feel like I have to work twice as hard to prove myself in everything." There's also a perception among students that Bridge is a program for "Polynesian kids" and "football players."*

And Punahou still has its blind spots. One alumnus recalled having to serve as an interpreter for her parents at school functions. "I think it was assumed that your parents could speak English. That was very different from my public school. . . . A lot of kids there had parents who were first-generation immigrants." Another student had a class project that required students to pay for postage. This student was saving every penny for summer program fees, and postage was not an expense she had budgeted for. She was initially hesitant to raise the issue.

*Casey Agena '94, "Bypass for a Leaky Educational Pipeline: A Case Study of the Bridge Program at Punahou School" (dissertation, Rossier School of Education, University of Southern California, 2011).

These may seem like minor details in the grand pursuit of access and diversity, but they send a message that students with less money are somehow not what Punahou expects or is designed to accommodate. Especially outside Bridge in the school at large, where there is no formal peer cohort or faculty support, a student of limited financial means can have a lonely experience. One recent alumnus, admitted on financial aid and now attending an Ivy League university, reflected on her Punahou experience and noted, "At Punahou, class wasn't really talked about. This helped because people didn't identify me as low income, but on the other hand, since it wasn't really talked about, it was hard to find students in situations like mine. It would have been nice if it was easier to find more students like me. Maybe also highlight faculty who were also low income or the first in their family to go to college."

Despite any shortcomings in Punahou's efforts, their positive impact is clear. Bridge students can explore a range of talents and interests at Punahou that might have gone untapped at a school with fewer offerings. "In middle school, I wasn't involved in extracurriculars," said one alumnus who attended Punahou on scholarship. "Then, coming to Punahou, I felt everyone was involved in something—dance, instruments, sports, community. It really forced me to look at what I wanted to do." And students leave Punahou prepared for college. A Bridge alumnus recalls, "[Bridge faculty] always talked about certain classes and clubs and sports that would be good for my college application. My parents didn't really know anything about that, but the teachers kept after me and my family."

By 2004, it seemed that Punahou was well on its way to answering the questions its president had raised a decade earlier. The fund-raising work of trustees and administrators had charted a course toward sustained financial aid. The Bridge Program and efforts like it were increasing the school's capacity to accommodate greater diversity. Important questions about means and capacity, though by no means settled, had formative answers. Yet deeper concerns, more difficult to articulate, still simmered even as the march toward a more diverse and accessible Punahou continued.

Twenty years after giving his address on access and diversity, Jim Scott opened Curriculum Day 2014 by declaring a new goal before the Punahou faculty. In another step toward greater access and diversity, Punahou would strive to cover 100 percent of demonstrated financial need for any student admitted whose family could not afford full tuition. In a sense, this was an extension of past efforts, since Punahou already covered 90 percent of demonstrated need. The move was

significant, however, because "full need" assistance would enable Punahou to admit students on a need-blind basis—ability to pay would not factor into admission decisions.

A large and unprecedented donation from Debbie Berger '82 and Bill Reeves, dedicated specifically to expanding economic access to Punahou School, supported the move. The couple had made the gift with the express hope that it would allow Punahou to admit talented students without financial consideration, freeing the admissions office to select a student body based on individual merit and an optimal mix for student learning. They also hoped that the community would embrace a more accessible and diverse Punahou as a valued partner, rather than viewing it as a separate and exclusive enclave.

By most accounts, initial faculty and staff reaction to the announcement was positive. For many, diversity—and, more specifically, financial aid—seemed a natural responsibility of Punahou as a well-heeled institution. "A place as resource rich as this, we should do it," said one teacher. Others found compelling purpose in serving underprivileged families: "To be able to extend spots to folks who wouldn't be thinking about Punahou—it's a worthy pursuit, especially for kids whose parents didn't go to college," said an administrator. Some saw an even greater benefit to society: "If someone didn't foot the bill for Obama's education, would he be president?"

However, the familiar notes of caution and concern, first raised after Scott's 1994 address, also resurfaced. "There's the notion that peers matter, even more than teachers or program," said one faculty member. "Part of what parents are paying for is to have their child surrounded by kids and families bent on success." An alumnus observed, "Some parents send their kids to Punahou for an entrée into a certain network," and wondered, "Will there be the same demand for Punahou if that changes?"

Punahou has long given preference to children of alumni in admissions. "So far," noted one administrator, "alumni are generally supportive of greater diversity. But if their kid is on the admissions bubble, it may be a different story." Punahou also gives preference to children of faculty and staff, children of Hawaiian descent, and descendants of members of the nineteenth-century Sandwich Islands Mission. Many wondered if Punahou would slaughter these sacred cows in a move toward need-blind admissions and full-need assistance.

Concerns about feasibility and capacity also persisted. The Bridge Program and other efforts represented important achievements, but they also underscored the investment required for success. If a student could not afford activity fees or camp supplies, would these be part of the aid package? Would the faculty have to engage in new forms of professional development?

Bishop Hall opened in 1972 as a technology-ready, state-of-the-art educational facility. Designed by architect Ernest Hara '28, Bishop Hall includes classrooms, Academy art studios, music studios, homemaking instructional facilities, and Bishop Learning Center, one of three libraries on campus. The Learning Center, with its large multi-media collection, serves students from grades five through eight.

Bishop Hall is named for philanthropist and Punahou trustee Charles R. Bishop, and is positioned on the site of the original Bishop Hall, built in 1901.

The sloped tile roof and plaster walls of the handsome and unpretentious Wo International Center, downslope from Bishop Hall on Chamberlain Drive, appear in the background. Mamiya Science Center, Sullivan Administration Building, and Wo International Center, all positioned along the entry drive and designed by John Hara '57, son of Ernest Hara, coherently reinforce Punahou's design tradition of dramatic, sloped tile-and-slate roofs combined with plaster facades.

Rice Field, often referred to as Middle Field, adjoins the spring and marks the center of campus. Named for William Harrison Rice and his wife, Mary Sophia Hyde Rice, the field is one of three on the Punahou campus that support athletic activities. Today, it is also the site of the annual Alumni Lūʻau.

The Rices taught at Punahou from 1844 to 1854 after completing their first posting, which was in Hāna, Maui. During the Rices' tenure at Punahou, the school grew much of the food served to boarding students and staff as a way to augment its meager budget. Mr. Rice was an agriculturalist and supervised the male boarders' fieldwork. They rose each school day at dawn to work amid the plots of corn, beans, bananas, watermelons, and squash. After supper, they returned to hoeing the fields "until it was dark enough to see two stars."

Mr. Rice, who oversaw the construction of two of the earliest buildings on campus, Rice Hall and Old School Hall, credited the boys' robust health to "exercise with their hoes." On the domestic side, Mrs. Rice, known as Mother Rice, experienced the repercussions of the boys' regime, writing that she "was expected to be a mother to ten or twelve boys with limited wardrobes, which required two days of the week for repairs."

In 1854, the Rices left Punahou, and William Harrison Rice became the manager of Lihue Plantation on Kauaʻi, a position he held until his death in 1863.

"Punahou's done a good job of being student centered in instruction," said one teacher, but another suggested, "We will need to think about increasing faculty diversity to match diversity in the student body."

The issue arose again of whether expanding access through financial aid would be counterproductive. Though Punahou tuition remains significantly lower than that of comparable day schools across the country, it has still risen even faster than inflation levels in Honolulu, a city with a perennially high cost of living. Some argued that while financial aid would make Punahou more accessible to qualified families, rising tuition could make the school less accessible overall. Proponents of expanding assistance were quick to point out that donations for financial aid would increase Punahou's endowment, the returns from which subsidize all students, since even full tuition covers only a portion of actual costs.

At times, the discussions that followed Scott's 2014 announcement were tense. The calls for caution from some quarters dismayed supporters of access and diversity. "I'm not sure where the hesitance is coming from," said one long-time advocate for greater diversity at Punahou. Those who questioned the investment in diversity were equally perplexed—no one wanted to be seen as "opposed to diversity," but many felt their concerns were being "glossed over," said a faculty member. One reason old worries resurfaced, even after more than twenty years of work in the interim, was that the diversity now proposed was of new and uncertain dimensions. Increasing aid for underprivileged applicants who represented a fraction of the student body was one thing. Rethinking admissions and "throwing open the gates," as Pennybacker put it, was something else—a scenario that promised a host of unknowns.

The rekindling of old concerns also revealed that the Punahou community had not resolved a more central question. Since 1994, supporters of access and diversity had commonly stated their case in terms of fairness, equity, "making Punahou representative of the community," and the "public purpose" of a prospering private school. Faculty and staff didn't resist such arguments—but not all found them compelling. Many of them expressed their unease with the question "What's in it for students?" Framing the commitment as a moral obligation did not answer this question directly. Though need-blind admission is more congruent with school values of meritocracy and educational excellence, the impact on quality of instruction remained an unknown. As one former faculty member opined, "Punahou should be focused on providing an excellent education to its students, regardless of how accessible it is or who gets preference in admissions."

This comment and others made two things clear. First, many of the concerns expressed stemmed from a deep commitment to teaching and learning, not an opposition to greater diversity at Punahou. Second, unless proponents could argue for access and diversity in terms of educational benefit for the school's students, rather than principally as a societal obligation, Punahou's efforts—no matter how noble—would continue to spawn as many questions as commitments from its faculty and staff.

At the time that Scott made his announcement in 2014, an answer to the question of "What's in it for students?" had already emerged. The work of teachers and students was demonstrating the answer, though it was never framed in terms of access and diversity. I discovered that answer, and the work that embodied it, when I reached out to a dozen recent graduates with two questions of my own.

My first question for young alumni was "Do you wish Punahou had been more diverse, and if so, why?" Each of the alumni I spoke with answered the question in the affirmative, and offered reasons that had less to do with social justice and more to do with their own learning.

One young woman felt that experiencing a greater variety of world views would have prepared her for one of the more difficult aspects of college. "The initial culture shock [of college] was the hardest part," she said. "All of a sudden there were people from all over the world, with different values than mine. I questioned a lot of things I'd never questioned before. . . . I was lost for a while. I almost came home."

Another alumnus recalled his experiences in higher education: "I learned significantly more from my study groups that had students from all over the country and the world . . . than from classroom instruction. Each person brought a different lens to the problem and, ultimately, how they chose to solve it. If we can bring some of this way of thinking and life experience to K–12 students, I think our islands and country will be better for it."

A third alumnus, who had graduated from college and started a career in communications, said: "I had to unlearn some of the habits I developed in school. I knew how to write for teachers and professors. It's harder to put yourself in the shoes of a more diverse audience and write for the public."

I asked two alumni if they would consider sending their own children to Punahou. One young woman, looking back at her own time at Punahou, said, "There was a lot of pressure for social performance. High school is already socially intense." She added that the homogeneity of Punahou made it feel "extra intense . . . like you faced exclusion if you didn't fit in." Noting that Punahou had recently declined admission to the shy child of a friend, she wondered, "If Punahou's only taking outgoing 'alpha' kids, what kind of environment is that creating?"

Another alumnus with young children said, "If everyone [at Punahou] is essentially on the path to college and becoming well rounded, how different are the students and their families from one another? As much as it pains me to see my own kids struggle with things, I know that struggle is the key to learning. Life does not guarantee that you will work with people like you. . . . If my kids aren't exposed to those challenges until college, it may be setting them up for failure in life."

It should be noted that none of these alumni expected Punahou to make them worldly and empathetic adults. They acknowledged that families and communities lay a critical foundation, and that life experiences ultimately teach a usable understanding of diversity. But they did observe how a homogeneous school environment, insulated from the rich diversity of its surroundings, could stunt students' growth in this regard and cause them to miss important learning opportunities.

My second question for alumni was "What was your most valuable experience at Punahou?" Here, the responses ranged more widely. Some pointed to teachers who had shaped them, while others recalled stories from camp or sports. A majority also referenced a different kind of experience, linked to the classroom but reaching beyond—into the community.

One recent graduate said that the Variety Show at the Punahou Carnival was her greatest learning experience at Punahou. It was "an opportunity for me to get involved in a project that brought so many different people together. . . . I worked with people I didn't know during my entire time at Punahou." She valued building new skills and relationships through countless rehearsals. The best part, she said, came when they exhibited their work in a Variety Show that reached a wide audience.

Another alumnus described a time some Punahou Academy students teamed up with a few public school student leaders to get high schoolers informed about, and involved in, the democratic process. With guidance from Punahou faculty at the Luke Center for Public Service and support from several local nonprofit organizations, the joint public-private school team organized "Pizza and Policy," an event at the Hawai'i State Capitol that drew more than 200 students from a dozen schools, with elected officials including the governor and house speaker on hand to meet directly with young participants.

A pair of alumni recounted their work on "DoBands"—a project that teamed Punahou students with students from Kealakehe High School, outside Kona. Adapting a concept from Stanford University, and supported by teachers and community organizations on both islands, the teams launched a joint experiment in "paying it forward." They produced and distributed wristbands marked with unique serial numbers, asking recipients to do a good deed, record it on a website, and then pass the band on. Anyone holding a band could go to the DoBands website, enter the band's number, and see its previous owners and their deeds. This project aimed to inspire a "wave of change, one good deed at a time."

Kealakehe students distributed bands to West Hawai'i residents and to tourists passing through Kona. Punahou students reached out through peers, friends, and family. The effort engaged hundreds of individuals, and the chain of good deeds eventually stretched across half a dozen states and countries. The project taught lessons in teamwork, long-distance collaboration, and communication, including "how different people responded differently to our message," remembered one alumnus. "What we were doing mattered to people—on the Big Island, on O'ahu, and eventually way beyond."

Finally, there was the story a recent graduate shared about a life-changing experience—a "Live Aloha" project, where students prepared and offered a free meal at a local beach park that was both a popular surf spot and a campground for many homeless families. Two things set the effort apart from a typical effort to feed the hungry. First, a local nonprofit supporting the effort challenged students to "reach across boundaries of culture, class, or neighborhood" through their event. Students would invite a mix of people to their meal—those who lived at the beach and those using it for recreation—and document the interactions and outcomes in a video. Second, Punahou students would step beyond their own boundaries by teaming with public school students living at a nearby homeless shelter to colead the project.

Cathy Kawano-Ching, the faculty mentor for the project, recalls that some of the students were taken aback at the first planning meeting, held at the shelter where their public school peers resided. "There was a lot of personal sharing...it was eye-opening." After that meeting, one Punahou student dropped out. "She showed a lot of self-awareness and courage," says Kawano-Ching, who is now the associate dean of Professional Programs at Punahou. "I don't think I'm ready for this," the freshman had said as they left the meeting.

The project proceeded with three homeless students and three Punahou students at the helm. Their event drew a mix of people to the table, feeding homeless and beachgoers alike, as planned. Punahou students shared their knowledge of videography, camera work, and editing with their public school co-organizers. Students from the shelter informed the method of out-reach and helped construct the storyboard in a way that recognized the worth of every voice captured.

The students also learned more personal lessons from each other. "I didn't think about some of the challenges they face as students," said a Punahou alumnus who had worked on the project as a junior. "With no desks at the shelter and no computers ... [and] shelter rules that require them to stay out until 5:30 but be back before 10 or stay out for the night," there were "serious limits on when we could get work done together."

Even more powerful were the stories their homeless peers shared. "The hardest part is when other kids don't know you're homeless and they start talking about homeless people," one homeless student said on camera. "I really learned a lot about what people think about home-lessness. They think it makes you a whole different person, but it doesn't." Another student shared his daily struggle to catch the bus to use library computers, and then get back to the shelter before doors closed for the night. "I couldn't get [my homework] done in time," he said. "My grades started going down. I started losing hope of going to college." A thirteen-year-old student living at the shelter said, "I'm tired of being a service project for other people. I want to be the one doing service."

"It changed the way I look at homeless people and the problem of homelessness," said a Punahou graduate. "It broadened my view of the world ... my perspective about my own life was different after that." And the freshman who dropped out initially? She returned to the shelter later as a junior and worked on projects there for the rest of her time at Punahou.

These experiences have certain features in common. Each was a valued opportunity to work with diverse peers on a project that had a real impact on the community. When the experience encompassed service, it was structured to create opportunities to learn both *with* and *from* those served, departing from the more familiar model of charity in which the giving goes in one direction only. In each instance, Punahou faculty acted more as facilitators than as instructors—shaping project parameters, identifying community partners, and structuring opportunities for mentoring, reflection, and peer learning.

The examples suggest one answer to the question "What's in it for students?" with a view of diversity as a benefit to all students, not only (or even principally) those on financial aid, and a vision of service as providing reciprocal rewards to communities and learners. Regarded in

this way, financial aid and the on-campus diversity it fosters are necessary to the preparation of young people for the world. Working with diverse peers can equip students to draw on different perspectives as they attempt to build successful families, companies, and communities.

These examples also illustrate the benefits of a Punahou "more reflective of and embraced by the community." Many of these learning experiences required partnerships with public schools and community organizations ranging from voter education programs to homeless shelters. Creating a perception of Punahou as more accessible and diverse is more than good public relations—it ensures that the wide range of community partners needed to craft powerful learning opportunities for students will welcome Punahou's presence.

A quarter century after Mindy Pennybacker assessed Punahou's standing as "the haole rich kids' school," it's clear that Punahou has gone beyond the "promising steps" she observed and taken some of the "great strides" she hoped for. At the same time, Punahou will have to move beyond the framework of aid, service, and public purpose as primary motives in its pursuit of access and diversity. These concepts have worth, but they miss one of the most compelling reasons for diversity—the life-changing learning opportunities it can offer students.

To create such an environment on its own campus, Punahou must be able to put students to work alongside peers with different life experiences, on projects that have meaning to the community. It must equip faculty to be facilitators, engaging a wide variety of partners in the process. And it must be accessible and useful to the community, not as a privileged giver, but as a participant in a two-way exchange of knowledge, moved by a spirit of reciprocity rather than one of noblesse oblige.

This approach will require the school to place itself in the role of learner, following the creative and courageous example of teachers and students already pioneering the work of learning from diversity. Punahou will need to place more trust in the diversity of Hawai'i as a teacher, drawing lessons from a community that traditionally blends different kinds of wisdom and offers a deep history of reciprocity. Then Punahou will do more than prepare its graduates for college; it will prepare them for a diverse world that demands adaptability. It will fulfill its promise as a school of the islands.

Beatrice Krauss's interest in plants and how Hawaiians used them began at an early age. As a child, she would accompany her father, University of Hawai'i agriculture professor Frederick Krauss, to the Mānoa campus, and in 1926 was the first woman to earn a degree in agriculture. In the late 1980s, when she was well into her eighties, Franco Salmoiraghi photographed Bea demonstrating how kapa is made.

Once wauke has been harvested, bark is stripped from the stalks and the fibrous inner bark is soaked and pounded until soft. With repeated beating and folding back onto itself, the kapa fabric becomes strong and pliable. Well-made kapa, bleached by the sun, is soft and creamy white and provides a luminous canvas for intricate designs.

BEATRICE H. KRAUSS 1922

BY GEORGE STAPLES

ei Day was something to look forward to, for it meant spending an early morning with Bea Krauss '22 examining the exquisite lei at Kapiʻolani Park. A newcomer who knew little about plants and their roles in the islands on arrival in 1988, I was truly fortunate to meet Bea through the city's annual Lei Day competition, where we helped out with the lei entry process as plant identifiers. Bea was a fountain of knowledge, and she enjoyed teasing the malihini (me) about what he didn't know. How we laughed! Then she would provide a private tutorial as we studied the lei and verified the names for the plants used to create them.

Like many people, I came to know Bea Krauss through her second career as a distinguished ethnobotanist—in fact, she was the doyenne of Hawaiian ethnobotany. After several of our Lei Day adventures, I drove her home, to the property in Mānoa where she had lived since childhood. Her father bought the two acres from Punahou School around 1909, and, except for a year of postgraduate study in Germany, Bea lived there her entire life.

While people still remember Bea for her ethnobotanical expertise and teaching, fewer know about her scientific career. After graduating from Punahou in 1922, she attended the University of Hawaiʻi, and in 1926 she was the first woman to receive a BS in agriculture from the young university. She joined the university's Pineapple Research Institute (PRI), where she spent her 42-year scientific career. That pineapples are grown so easily today as a global commercial crop owes much to the research of the PRI crop scientists. The observation in Hawaiʻi (and elsewhere) that smoke drifting from burning sugarcane fields nearby caused the pineapples to flower synchronously opened a line of investigation that ultimately led to understanding how to manipulate fruit production and make pineapple harvesting vastly more efficient.

Bea traveled to the Azores to study pineapple growers' use of smoking to force flowering and fruit production—a technique that allowed them to produce pineapples out of season, when they brought a higher price. Her detailed report in 1940 set the stage for the investigations by PRI plant physiologists, which led to the discovery years later that a plant growth hormone stimulated this flowering. No one remembers this foundational crop

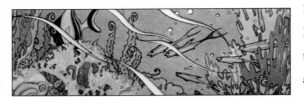

science research today, and Bea Krauss's role in it has been likewise forgotten.

Instead, she is fondly remembered for her teaching in the field of Hawaiian ethnobotany, a second career she began after retiring from the PRI in 1968. The Hawaiian Renaissance was just starting, and its proponents took tremendous interest in all dimensions of traditional Hawaiian knowledge, including the use of plants. For six years Bea taught at the university, where students flocked to her classes. Then she continued her instruction at the Lyon Arboretum, University of Hawaiʻi at Mānoa, where she was a research associate starting in 1973. After retiring from the arboretum in 1983, she used her lecture notes and class syllabi as the foundation of her two best-known books: *Plants in Hawaiian Culture* (1994) and *Plants in Hawaiian Medicine* (2001).

In 1975, Bea started a garden at the Lyon Arboretum devoted to plants traditionally used in Hawaiʻi. Today, the Beatrice H. Krauss Hawaiian Ethnobotanical Garden is a serene and lovely spot, a living testament to her many contributions to Hawaiʻi and Hawaiian cultural knowledge. Bea Krauss left us an amazing legacy as a scientist, teacher, and champion of traditional knowledge, and she graciously and generously shared her gifts.

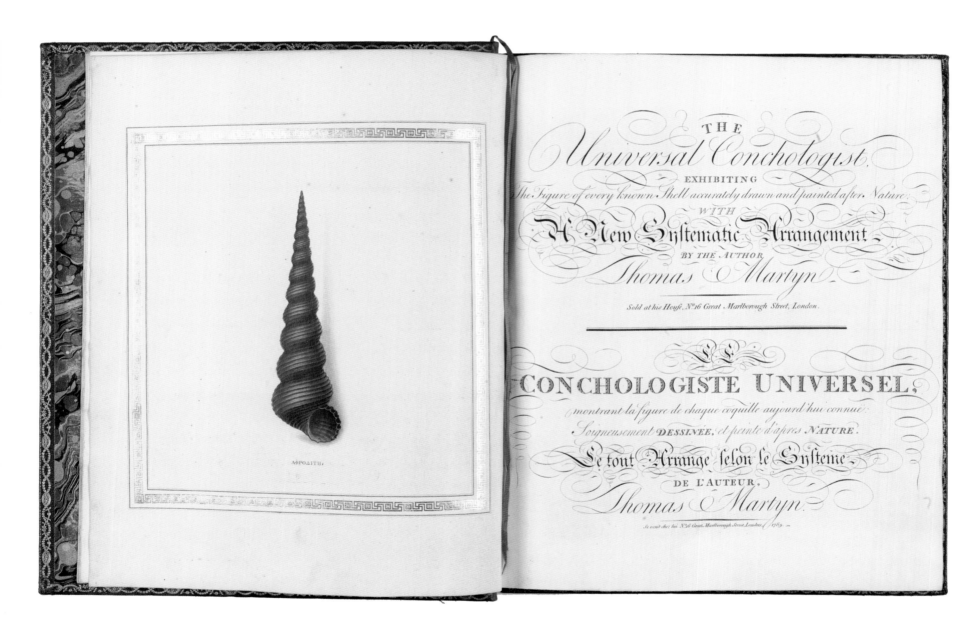

Alison Kay traveled the world to study shells, both in their natural habitats and in scientific collections. The rare and beautiful book shown here, published in 1789 and titled The Universal Conchologist, Exhibiting the Figure of Every Known Shell Accurately Drawn and Painted after Nature, was of great interest to her because it includes exquisite renderings of shells collected on Captain James Cook's three voyages, including specimens identified as having been obtained in the Hawaiian Islands.

E. ALISON KAY 1946

BY JULIA STEELE

EAlison Kay '46 grew up on Kaua'i in the 1930s, swimming and bodysurfing at Brennecke's Beach and combing the sands of Po'ipū, Māhā'ulepū, and Kukui-'ula. Those idyllic days of exploring the shore and collecting shells shaped the course of her life, though it would be a few years before she realized just how profoundly. When she was a senior at Mills College in Oakland, California, her biology teacher noticed her love of shells and suggested that she study malacology. Up to that point Alison had intended to be a physician, but in that moment she decided that shells were her calling.

She went to Cambridge University and earned a BA cum laude in 1952 and an MA in 1956, and then returned to the University of Hawai'i at Mānoa, from which she received her PhD for a thesis on the family of Cypraeidae: cowries, her first love. Alison's life remained closely tied to the Mānoa campus from that point on. In 1962 the university hired her as a professor in the Department of General Science, where, along with botanist Dr. Charles Lamoureux, she taught an iconic Hawaiian natural history course. Alison wanted everyone to celebrate the wonders of the natural world, recalls her colleague Sheila Conant: "She always thought it was really important that everyone

The 1946 Oahuan *includes this charming senior portrait of E. Alison Kay. Born and raised on Kaua'i, she left the islands to attend Mills College and Cambridge University. She returned to earn a PhD at the University of Hawai'i at Mānoa and is known for her major work,* Hawaiian Marine Shells.

should not be afraid of science. She had tremendous enthusiasm and high expectations of the students."

Her four years at Punahou shaped Alison's appreciation for good teaching. Her parents were Scottish immigrants who had come to Kaua'i so her father could take a job at one of the island's

sugar mills. After his death, Alison moved to O'ahu with her mother and brother, and she attended Punahou from 1942 to 1946. Her first three years at the school coincided with World War II, when the Army Corps of Engineers took over the Punahou campus, forcing the school to move its classes to private homes and the University of Hawai'i's Wist Hall. When she graduated, the 1946 *Oahuan* carried this description: "Always reliable —that's Alison. This blonde, blue-eyed Kauai-ite is a great swimming enthusiast and excels in this sport as well as everything she undertakes."

"The great thing that Punahou taught me how to do was write an essay, a senior theme," recalled Alison in the 1990s. "I could not have handled . . . Cambridge without that senior theme." The writing was a lifelong affair: She published numerous papers throughout her career and a number of books, including, in 1979, her major work, the authoritative *Hawaiian Marine Shells*. Her specialty was mollusks; in addition to studying cowries, she focused on micromollusks, tiny creatures that she showed could act as an indicator species for biomonitoring. Fabio Moretzsohn, the final graduate student she advised (he received his PhD in 2003), remembers Alison telling a story of finding, in the recesses of a European museum, a sand sample that Captain James Cook had collected in the shallow waters off Waikīkī. Alison went through it, picked out the micromollusks, counted them, and replaced them. She then sampled the same area and discovered, to her happiness, that the count had remained quite similar. At least six shells have been named in her honor, including a cowrie, *Cypraea alisonae*.

Alison traveled the world to study shells. Every summer she headed to the Natural History Museum in London to work; her research spots in the field included Enewetak Atoll, where she became the first female scientist to set foot on the island after challenging the rules of the Atomic Energy Commission. At the University of Hawaiʻi, she was a tireless advocate for graduate students; she served as dean of the Graduate Division after moving to the Zoology Department. In the community, she lobbied for the protection of Diamond Head and, proud of her heritage, joined the local Scottish society. When she died in 2008, her memorial service featured a portrait of her and, next to it, a picture of *Cypraea alisonae* and a bottle of fifteen-year-old Scotch whisky. "Her legacy is her students," notes Regina Kawamoto of the Bernice Pauahi Bishop Museum, who worked alongside Alison for thirty years. "She treated her students like family."

opposite

Swimming is Punahou's oldest sport, dating to the mid-1880s. Early students trained in a 47-foot cement swimming tank and competed against community members, including Duke Kahanamoku. The current, Olympic-sized pool was built in 1981, replacing the original 75-by-35-foot pool that was built in 1922. Each year more than 2,500 students use the Elizabeth P. Waterhouse Memorial Swimming Pool.

The C. Dudley Pratt Aquatic Center comprises the Elizabeth P. Waterhouse Pool and facilities that support the school's aquatics program. The Center is named for C. Dudley Pratt (1918), a champion swimmer, dedicated public servant, and school trustee from 1943 to 1970. At the Center's dedication in 1981, former teacher and legendary swimmer Pete Powlison '40 dove into the pool and swam a 50-meter lap before a cheering crowd. Powlison was a Punahou trustee from 1986 to 1987.

The pool is named in memory of Elizabeth P. Waterhouse (1922), who was a swimmer during her years at Punahou. Her parents, John (1892) and Martha Alexander Waterhouse, provided funds for construction of the original pool in 1922. John Waterhouse served as a school trustee from 1914 to 1941.

The Pratt Aquatic Center and the current Waterhouse Pool are part of the physical education and athletics complex designed by architects Ernest Hara '28 and John Hara '57 and completed in 1981.

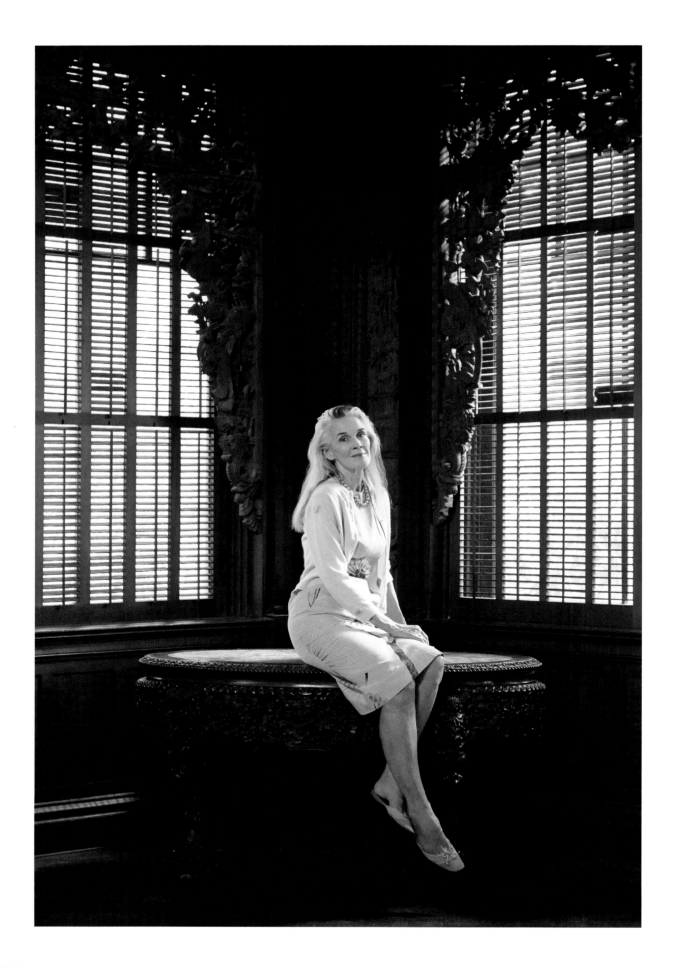

A WAVE OF WOMEN WRITERS

BY JULIA FLYNN SILER

A Korean refugee forced into prostitution. A synagogue in Honolulu reeling after its president disappears with funds. A family descended from Hawaiian royalty and Christian missionaries facing a decision to sell land. A girl's surprisingly intimate surfing lesson with a Waikīkī beach boy.

A powerful wave of women writers from Punahou has explored these and other subjects in recent decades. They are some of Hawai'i's—and the nation's—most admired fiction writers. They've won prestigious prizes, seen their books turned into films, and written *New York Times* bestsellers. Their influence and their concerns range far beyond the Hawaiian Islands. What Nora Okja Keller, Allegra Goodman, Kaui Hart Hemmings, and Susanna Moore all have in common is that they learned some of their earliest lessons about writing and about life at their shared alma mater.

Two of these writers developed a lifelong perspective as outsiders. The other two found love and refuge at the school and, later in their professional lives, supported each other's work. Although they graduated years or even decades apart, each woman had teachers at Punahou who helped convince her that she had the curiosity and sensitivity to become a writer.

Susanna Moore
1963

Nora Okja Cobb Keller
1983

Allegra Goodman
1985

Kaui Hart Hemmings
1994

opposite
Novelist Susanna Moore in the Chinese Pavilion at Moanalua Gardens. After living away from Hawai'i for nearly fifty years, Susanna returned home in 2013. She lives in North Kohala on the island of Hawai'i and teaches creative writing each fall at Princeton University. Her most recent work is a history of nineteenth-century Hawai'i.

Nora Okja Cobb '83 Keller, who won an American Book Award for her powerful debut novel, *Comfort Woman* (Viking Penguin, 1997), arrived at Punahou in 1977 as a scholarship student in the seventh grade. Commuting an hour and a half each way from Waimānalo, she helped finance her tuition through a work-study program. Although initially she felt like an outsider, she eventually returned to the school and now teaches English in the Academy. She is also a parent with two daughters at the school.

"It's funny," says the Korean-American author and teacher, sitting in her classroom. "I never thought I would be back at Punahou." She credits her teachers for helping her overcome her shyness and learn how to express herself in public. "It was very difficult to come from a background where you didn't speak out and to learn to tell your own stories," she recalls.

In her review of *Comfort Woman* in the *New York Times,* Michiko Kakutani praised it as "a powerful book about mothers and daughters and the passions that bind one generation to another. It is a book that combines the familial intimacy of Louise Erdrich's early novels with the fierce, historical magic of Toni Morrison's *Beloved*." Nora's second book, *Fox Girl* (Penguin, 2003), explores some of the same themes, also with devastating subtlety. Both of her books, Keller explains, "explore how we carry history with us."

Allegra Goodman '85, who entered Punahou in kindergarten, says she too felt like an outsider much of the time. Her sense of otherness came from being one of the few Jewish students at Punahou at that time. Because of her very fair skin, she

Nora Okja Keller, photographed in New York upon the release of her novel, Comfort Women.

Allegra Goodman's Punahou high school teacher, William Messer,
inspired her love of Elizabethan literature and spurred her to write
cogent critical essays. She began writing short stories in high school,
and the summer after she graduated in 1985, submitted the story
"Variant Text" to Commentary magazine, hoping that the editors
wouldn't realize that she was only seventeen. The day she graduated
from Harvard in 1989 was the day her first book was published.

Kaui Hart Hemmings lives and writes in Maunawili Valley on O'ahu. Her 2015 book, Juniors, *a young adult novel set at Punahou, explores the dynamic between mothers and daughters and the struggles of high school students.*

Kaui attended Punahou from kindergarten to graduation and she recalls being "a semi-disruptive, argumentative, attention-seeking, and sassy student." Within the acknowledgements to her new book, she thanked her teachers at Punahou, "...for some reason you interpreted my antics as creative, funny, and unique, thank you—those words are so much better. Your support was palpable and motivational—it made me want to prove you were right."

recalls, "People would come up to me and say, 'Why are you so white?' It made me pretty miserable, and I haven't forgotten it all these years."

But she also has happy memories from her Punahou years, including the encouragement she got from people like her second-grade teacher, Mrs. June Brieske, who helped her produce a bound version of her fanciful story about a train that danced a jig to make a fairy-tale princess laugh. "That was my very first book," she says. Her novel *Intuition* (Dial Press, 2007) became a *New York Times* best seller, and her first novel, *Kaaterskill Falls* (Dial Press, 1998), was a National Book Award finalist. Another of her books, *The Family Markowitz* (Farrar, Straus and Giroux, 1998), began as a series of short stories published in the *New Yorker.*

Allegra combines a gift for close observation with astute psychological insight, prompting reviewers to compare her to a modern-day Jane Austen. NPR book critic Maureen Corrigan, reviewing *Intuition*, a novel set in a research lab, described her as a "literary miniaturist who keeps slowly rotating the focus until a seething cosmos emerges under her lens." A prolific novelist, Allegra's eighth book is due out in 2017. She is also the mother of four children and lives in Cambridge, Massachusetts.

Susanna Moore '63 attended Punahou from second grade until she graduated at 17. She says the school influenced her profoundly, in part because she didn't go on to college, so Punahou was her sole experience of formal education. The school helped her get through a traumatic period at age 12, when her mother died. "They were indulgent and kind, and I don't think it was just for me," she says, recalling that Punahou became a refuge where she was "infinitely encouraged."

Her childhood, which largely overlapped with her time at the school, became a rich source of literary inspiration. She later explored in her books the notion of Punahou as part of a neocolonial world of privilege she had lived in as a schoolgirl. Joyce Carol Oates, writing in the *New York Review of Books*, described Susanna's novel set in Hawai'i, *My Old Sweetheart* (Houghton Mifflin, 1982), as "an elegiac reminiscence of an island childhood ... one of those elusive, shimmering works of fiction, bold, impressionistic, subtle, and mysterious, that resist paraphrase and summary."

Romance and longing infuse Susanna's memory of her experiences at Punahou. Her first true love was her fifth-grade teacher, then a recent Williams College graduate, who later disappeared—and presumably died—during a dugout canoe expedition in Papua New Guinea. She left Hawai'i for the continental United States the day after she graduated from Punahou, and eventually became its leading expatriate writer. Her novel set in New York, *In the Cut* (Alfred A. Knopf, 1995), was made into a movie directed by Jane Campion and starring Meg Ryan, and in 1999 she received an award for literary achievement from the American Academy of Arts and Letters. In 2013, after residing for many years in New York and elsewhere, Susanna moved back to Hawai'i to marry fellow Punahou alumnus William S. Chillingworth '61. Her most recent book, *Paradise of the Pacific*, is a richly documented history of nineteenth-century Hawai'i built upon unfiltered personal accounts, including letters and diaries of men and women in the Protestant missionary community in Hawai'i.

Kauikeolani Hart Hemmings '94, who entered Punahou in kindergarten in 1981, also spent time living on the continent before returning to Hawai'i, as did Susanna Moore and Nora Keller. One of her most vivid memories of the school is Mrs. Joan Florence-Van Dyke's sixth-grade English class, where she recalls acting the part of the class clown and provocatively including swear words in the stories she wrote. She remembers "Flo" telling her, "You don't have to pretend to be dumb."

Those words sank in, and Kaui, who is Native Hawaiian, went on to win a prestigious Wallace Stegner Fellowship at Stanford University and to write the novel *The Descendants* (Random House, 2007), a *New York Times* best seller that was made into an Oscar-winning film directed by Alexander Payne and starring George Clooney. Like Susanna Moore, Kaui examined the world of Hawai'i's elite, but she channeled the wry sense of humor that once made her the class clown into a poignantly funny look at painful subjects, such as substance abuse, infidelity, and land use in Hawai'i. A review of *The Descendants* in the *New York Times* noted, "Her comic sense is finely honed in this refreshingly wry debut novel."

Kaui and Susanna—though separated by several decades in age and worldview—have become friends and literary colleagues. Both are grateful to the school for their early educations as writers. Kaui noted that both Susanna and Allegra were inspirational to her, "I've always loved and admired both of them for being able to write in a fictional way about the place they grew up, and then for…writing about something else." Kaui's latest work, *Juniors*, published in 2015, is a young adult novel set at Punahou.

opposite

White bird-of-paradise is planted along the facade of Dillingham Hall facing Chamberlain Drive. The white flowers and gray-green, waxy-coated leaves echo the ivory-colored plaster walls and the glazed, green-colored tiles on the building roof.

Mrs. Mabel Hefty's 1972 fifth-grade class.

BARACK OBAMA 1979

BY ALLEGRA GOODMAN '85

In the winter of 2007–08, Barack Obama '79 was a young candidate running for US president. He was not as experienced or as well known as his rivals—he was certainly not the front-runner at that time. In December 2007, an editor from *The New Republic* asked me to write a short essay about Obama's connection to Hawai'i and to Punahou School (published February 13, 2008, and reprinted here with permission). While I had never met Obama at Punahou, I discovered that we had shared some of the same teachers. Mabel Hefty, his fifth-grade teacher and mine, was someone I remembered well. Mrs. Hefty was nothing if not consistent, and so I knew some of the lessons the future president had learned in her class.

Rainbow Warrior

My fifth-grade classroom at Punahou, a private school in Honolulu founded by nineteenth-century Congregational missionaries, was on the third floor of Castle Hall, in an airy room with big windows that Mrs. Hefty covered with blackout curtains when she showed us films. We thought nothing of the room-darkening curtains, until one day Mrs. Hefty explained to us that they were left over from curfew after Pearl Harbor, when every-

one feared the Japanese would come back to bomb O'ahu again. A veteran teacher, old-fashioned, Christian, strict, Mabel Hefty wasn't shy about imparting history. Not one to tolerate pidgin English in her class, she insisted that each of us learn to recite Psalm 23 in the King James Version. Never one to ignore politics, she wore orange on St. Patrick's Day, because, as she explained to us, she sided with the English in Ireland. Her voice was matter of fact; her manner old-school. When she taught sex ed, she stood before our class of ten-year-olds and knit her fingers together to show what it was like when a man and a woman came together, wanting a baby. Nobody laughed.

Six years before she taught my class, Mabel Hefty had taught a boy named Barack Obama who grew up to name her as his favorite teacher for her ability to make "every single child feel special." To Mrs. Hefty, special did not simply mean loved—special meant singular. This was a particularly

strong message to her diverse students. Mrs. Hefty's students were Chinese, Japanese, Hawaiian, Korean, Tongan, white, and, more often than that, hapa, a combination of many races and traditions. On the surface, our classroom looked like a melting pot. A girl with honey-blond hair, café au lait skin, and green eyes might say proudly, "I'm part Hawaiian, part Portuguese, part Chinese, and part Irish." And yet, despite this melding of cultures—indeed, because of it—we were all struggling to define ourselves and find a place in the world. What did it mean to live in Hawai'i—especially for those of us who had no native Hawaiian ancestry? Were we immigrants? Invaders? Americans? These questions now frame Obama's campaign.

Obama is a singular presidential candidate, a galvanizing force for the younger generation of Democrats and independents. He's had a short political life—necessarily scant in accomplishments and compromises, and rich in symbolism. He speaks as a man with an unusual personal history: "My father . . . grew up herding goats . . . my mother . . . was born in a town on the other side of the world, in Kansas." He speaks as a newcomer, an achiever, the embodiment of the American dream. His story excites his audiences, as does his savvy understanding of a historical moment in

Castle Hall, built in 1913, was initially home to female boarding students from the neighbor islands and then a central location for fourth-, fifth-, and sixth-grade Junior School classes.

A gift from Mary Tenney Castle in honor of her husband Samuel N. Castle, one of Punahou's founding trustees, provided for the construction of a girls' dormitory in 1907. A fire in 1911 destroyed the wooden hall, and the decision was made to rebuild in concrete. The opportunity to rebuild the dormitory was due, again, to the generousity of the Castle family. The neoclassical building in a restrained Beaux-Arts style was designed by Emory & Webb, a leading architectural firm in Honolulu.

Boarders affectionately called Castle Hall the "Hash House." The girls gathered every Friday afternoon for tea, where darning advice was dispensed along with refreshments. When football season came around "the 'hash house' was the center of the excitement, for the boys ate their training lunches there, with all the boarders crowding around the heroes," wrote Mary Alexander (1892) and Charlotte Dodge (1902). Punahou ended its boarding program in 1963.

which mainland America seems poised to catch up to the Hawai'i of his youth.

To envision a world where racial identity is more fluid, where men and women are more mobile, and where segregation is a thing of the past is not to envision a postracial world. Obama knows this, as anyone who has lived in Hawai'i must. The lovely tropical home of so many diverse people is not beyond distinctions—it is all about them. Tensions simmer between Native Hawaiians and newcomers. The rich layered cultures of Polynesia, Asia, and America bump up against bigotry and ignorance, often voiced in racist jokes and sometimes expressed in physical violence. Punahou's student body is multicultural and its financial aid generous. But for some, Punahou symbolizes exclusive privilege. More than once when I was a student there, rough kids from outside breached the walls. Teachers sounded the alarm: "The mokes are on campus again"—the word "mokes" designating kids who were native and poor. They'd come with pipes or with their fists and scare a few students and administrators, but sporadic displays of anger were no match for Punahou, with its wealth of resources and manicured grounds. The kids' protest was sad, and the gap between their opportunities and ours was sadder.

Honolulu is no utopia; its socioeconomic climate is far from Edenic. However, Honolulu's complexity and diversity are great gifts for a reflective future leader. To grow up in Hawai'i is to see the United States from the inside and the outside. The inside view comes from pride in statehood and military tradition. Long before September 11, residents of Hawai'i knew what foreign attack was like and valued American protection—Pearl Harbor remains a vital piece of Hawai'i's history. The outside view of the United States comes from geographic distance. The Hawaiian Islands stand as tiny meeting points for immigrants from Japan, China, Korea, the Philippines, and the far reaches of Polynesia. Hawai'i is an outpost among many nations, not a state connected by highways to other states. As a meeting place, the islands are cosmopolitan. As an isolated island chain, the islands are also parochial. The haves in Hawai'i travel and see the world. The have-nots, many of them Native Hawaiians, lack the means to get away. To grow up in Hawai'i is to envision the future of a multiracial society, and also to view up close the disappointment of those left behind.

How will Obama convert his colorful background into action? How will his Hawaiian experience with race and class inform his decisions? It's impossible to say now. But Obama did have Mrs. Hefty's endorsement. Before she died, Mrs. Hefty reportedly told her daughter, "I know he's going to be somebody." Who would Obama be? For a start, perhaps, he would become a little like his favorite teacher. Shrewd and dramatic, he would mesmerize audiences with his confidence in his own story. He would speak of his background without apology, and without notes. He'd strive to make each voter feel special. He would always remember his time at Punahou. And he would know Psalm 23, with its credo of private conviction and public destiny: "The Lord is my shepherd; I shall not want…Thou preparest a table before me in the presence of mine enemies: Thou anointest my head with oil…" He'd know those lines by heart.

opposite

In 1990, Barack Obama was elected president of the Harvard Law Review, the first Black law student to hold the title in the 104-year history of the Review. Prior to enrolling at Harvard Law School, Obama attended Occidental College in Los Angeles, graduated from Columbia University in New York, and spent four years working as a community organizer on Chicago's South Side.

The Review editors were a contentious group, and classmate Brad Berenson, Supreme Court editor of the Harvard Law Review (who went on to work in the George W. Bush White House) noted, "To portray him [Obama] as someone who brought everyone together wouldn't be accurate, but he was a non-combatant. He was mature and held himself above the fray. He was courteous, decent, and respectful, even toward conservatives, who were a distinct minority on the Law Review staff."

136

In 1916, President Arthur F. Griffiths engaged New York-based architect Bertram Goodhue to develop a campus master plan. Goodhue with his first partner, Ralph A. Cram, had designed several buildings for Princeton University in the early 1900s.

Goodhue had recently completed his commission as the advisory and consulting architect for the plan of the landmark San Diego Exposition in Balboa Park, 1915–1917. His work at Balboa Park, including his design of the California Building, gave birth to what became known as Spanish Colonial Revival architecture, still associated with California and the southwest today. But, following his work in Balboa Park for the San Diego Exposition, Goodhue moved decisively toward greater simplicity in his architecture, paring away unnecessary ornamentation.

Goodhue's master plan for Punahou, accepted in 1920, emphasized many of the distinctive features that continue to define the campus today. His plan indicated sites for future buildings, including Dillingham Hall, which he began designing while working on the master plan. Goodhue noted that the simplicity of "the old schoolhouse" should inspire a simplicity of approach for future buildings on the campus.

Dillingham Hall, completed in 1929, is a study in classic volumes and proportions, steeped roofs, stucco walls, and simply ornamented, sheltered outdoor spaces. Spanish Colonial influences can be seen in the building's tiled roof, exposed beams, and carved wooden roof supports. Architect Goodhue also designed the Honolulu Academy of Arts, which opened in 1927, one of the finest examples of an architectural style suited to the islands.

Contemporary architect John Hara, designer of several campus buildings, including Sullivan Administraton Building and Mamiya Science Center flanking Dillingham Hall, has achieved a modern continuity to Goodhue's sensibilities through his masterful handling of proportion and roofs as essential architectural elements.

opposite
The Punahou campus, as depicted in a 1917 map drawn by Baldwin and Alexander, shows many of the components that Goodhue incorporated into and emphasized in his 1920 campus master plan— an axis that runs perpendicular to Punahou Street, a focus on open space, and the central importance of the spring.

Although the map shows an array of buildings different from today's campus, it identifies trees that continue to grace Kapunahou, including the royal poinciana trees that line the upper edge of Alexander Field, the tamarind tree near old Bingham Hall (which was replaced by Alexander Hall in 1933), and the royal palms along Palm Drive.

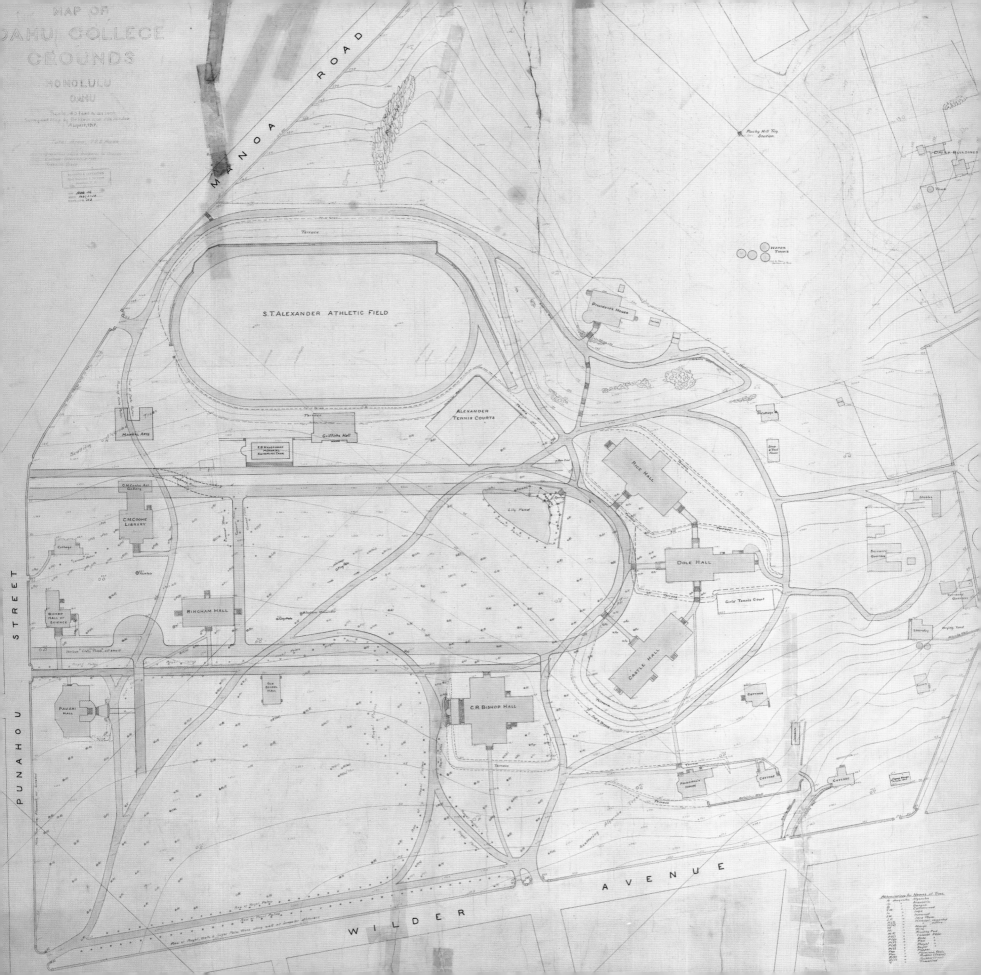

Dillingham Hall was a gift from Benjamin F. and Emma L. Smith (1863) Dillingham to celebrate Punahou's 75th anniversary jubilee in 1916 and to provide the school with an assembly hall for its growing student body. World War I interrupted plans for construction, and the building was not completed until 1929. Today, Dillingham Hall continues to serve as an assembly space for students and as the performance center for Punahou's theater, music, and dance programs.

B. F. Dillingham was the founder of Oahu Railway and Land Company, which built a railway from Honolulu to Waialua and Wai'anae. His son, Walter F. (1889), served as a Punahou trustee from 1904 to 1964.

Dillingham Hall has long been known for the quality of its acoustics. Mahi Beamer, Hawaiian tenor falsetto extraordinaire, chose Dillingham to record his two now-classic recordings featuring the music of his grandmother, Helen Desha Beamer, in 1959, and classical violinist Eugene Fodor praised the acoustic qualities of Dillingham following his performance in 1985.

143

Students from the class of 2014 gear up for their Variety Show, a Carnival tradition that showcases diverse talents. Beyond entertainment, Variety Show brings members of the senior class together—including orchestra member Leigh Johnston '14 — as they enter their final months of school.

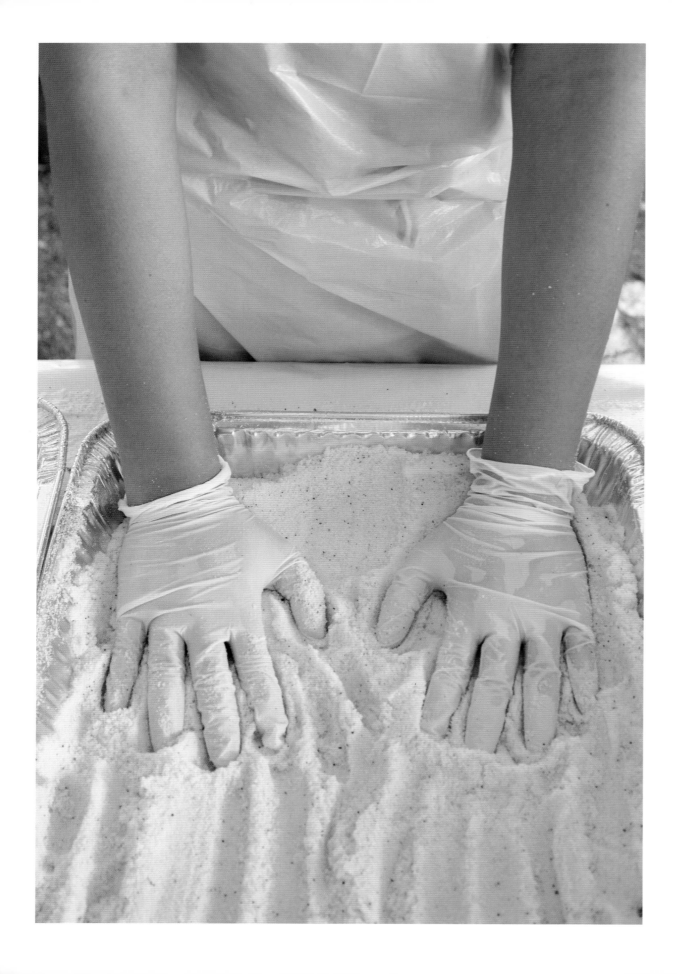

The Punahou Carnival began in 1932 as an effort by the senior class to raise funds for their yearbook. Today, the Junior Class coordinates yearlong preparations for the two-day event, proceeds of which support the school's financial aid program. The school welcomes the broader community onto campus each year to enjoy Carnival rides, games and distinctive treats.

GLOBAL LEARNING

SARA LIN '99

I n 1989, Punahou received a tremendous donation from the families of C. S. Wo and K. J. Luke to build an international center. At the time, it was the biggest gift in the school's history. With a great donation comes great responsibility. The Wo family, led by brothers Jim Wo '43 and Bob Wo '41, gave the money out of concern that their grandchildren's generation needed a whole new level of preparation to succeed in a globally integrated economy. Punahou already boasted a slate of international and study abroad programs, thanks to the efforts of a few pioneering educators. Still, the Wo brothers hoped that the new center would be a catalyst for the development of even more international programs.

The Wo International Center, and the Luke Center for Chinese Studies and Luke Lecture Hall sited within it, offered dedicated space and resources for the school's burgeoning international programs. The planning process for the center also gave immediacy to an ongoing discussion among administrators and educators about how Punahou can prepare students for a world that is becoming more interconnected everyday. What does it mean to be a global citizen? Is it enough to learn another language, or do today's students need to do more than that to be globally competent? And how do programs that began as summer electives evolve to become more central to the teaching and learning experience?

Administrators faced a twofold challenge: building the center itself, and then nurturing programs that would help the center fulfill its purpose. Addressing these issues was the life's work of a team of educators, in particular two visionaries: Siegfried Ramler, the founding director of the Wo International Center, and Hope Kuo Staab, who led the center for fifteen years. Under their tenures, global education became a core part of the school's educational mission. The Wo Center established itself as a model for global education, and, thanks in part to the center's reputation, Punahou gained recognition as a leading figure in education.

Any conversation about global education at Punahou begins with Siegfried Ramler. An Austrian by birth, Ramler moved to Hawai'i in 1949 as a newlywed, having met his future wife, Hawai'i native Pi'ilani Ahuna, at the Nuremberg trials of Nazi war criminals, where Ahuna was a court reporter and Ramler an interpreter and translator. Two years after coming to Hawai'i, he accepted a job teaching German and French at Punahou. Ramler formalized foreign language instruction at Punahou, organizing teachers into a department and over the years expanding language offerings from two years of French and Latin to six years of Japanese, Chinese, Spanish, French, and German. He also organized meaningful experiences to complement students'

language studies, such as summer trips abroad, many including home stays with host families.

Punahou could not have asked for a more dynamic person to spearhead its international outreach. Ramler's experiences during the Second World War and the complex international trials that took place afterward gave him an acute perspective on the importance of cross-cultural understanding and global awareness. As a Jewish teenager, Ramler was living in Nazi-annexed Vienna. He was fourteen years old when Great Britain's Kindertransport rescue mission evacuated him. He experienced the war years in London and lived through the German air raids. Later, while acting as an interpreter at the Nuremberg trials, he helped develop a simultaneous translation system that enabled listeners to hear court proceedings in four languages: English, German, Russian, and French.

Ramler brought that inventive spirit with him to Punahou, where he relentlessly pushed for new international opportunities for his students. "I felt strongly that Punahou, although independent in its governance, should not isolate itself behind the walls and hedges surrounding the 80 acres of the campus, but should commit itself to its public purpose and responsibility, both in Hawai'i and beyond," he wrote in his 2008 memoir, *Nuremberg and Beyond*.

Several of the earliest student exchanges that Ramler created made history. In the summer of 1978, one year before the United States reopened diplomatic relations with China, Ramler led one of the first visits from a US school to China since the pre-Mao era. His brainchild, the Pan Pacific Program, is a summer program for approximately 30 students from Asia, Southeast Asia, and the Pacific that began as a partnership in 1969 between Punahou School and the Keio Schools in Japan. To date, it remains the longest-lasting Japanese-American exchange program in the history of both countries. The Pan Pacific Program has grown to include students from other countries, including Cambodia, China, Taiwan, Malaysia, Indonesia, the Philippines, Tahiti, Thailand, and Vietnam. Students improve their English language skills while also learning about Hawaiian culture, and study science by examining Hawai'i's environment.

For years, Ramler ran these programs out of a tiny office in the back of Cooke Library. The Pan Pacific Program, although based at Punahou, was not officially part of the curriculum, and was administered through the Foundation for Study in Hawaii and Abroad, an independent nonprofit organization founded by Ramler. The Wo International Center, dedicated in 1993, incorporated Ramler's programs and Punahou named him the center's first director, placing him at the forefront of the school's efforts to craft a new vision for global education.

The Wo International Center is a handsome white building, carved into the grassy hillside next to Bishop Hall, where kids once slid on cardboard boxes. Designed by Honolulu architect John Hara '57, the center echoes the profile of the nearby Sullivan Administration Building, drawing on Mediterranean and Mission revival architecture styles prominent in Hawai'i during the territorial period. The Wo Center gave Punahou's international programs a physical base and a sense of permanence, ensuring that Ramler's initiatives would survive beyond his tenure. The significance of his contributions cannot be overstated: Early on, he recognized that Punahou needed to expose its students to international experiences beyond studying a foreign language. Still, even after the Wo Center opened, travel and student exchange programs remained elective add-ons rather than integrated parts of the academic curriculum.

Weaving the international programs into the broader mission of the school were tasks for the next generation. When Ramler stepped down in 1995, Academy teachers Bob Torrey and Hope Kuo Staab took over as codirectors. The two worked on developing deeper connections between the Wo Center and the rest of the campus while also adding more programs. Torrey, a historian and Fulbright scholar, expanded outreach to Latin America, Europe, and the Middle East, while Staab focused on Asia and the Pacific. Three years later, Staab took over as sole director, a position she held for fifteen years before stepping down to return to the classroom. She passed away in February 2014.

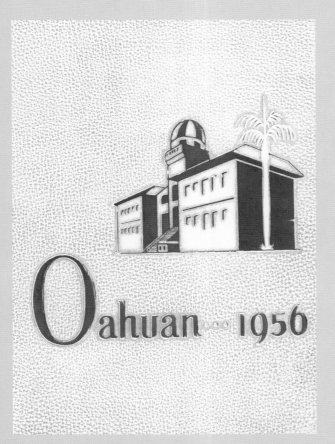

Hope Kuo Staab was born in Taiwan and grew up in Korea, Samoa, and Fiji, though her first language was Mandarin. Her family moved often due to her father's work as a doctor with the World Health Organization. Those early experiences abroad shaped a lifelong passion for learning about other cultures. She attended the University of Kansas, where she double-majored in linguistics and East Asian studies. She earned a master's degree in English as a second language at the University of Hawai'i at Mānoa, and later went back for a second master's in Chinese linguistics. In 1976, her first year of teaching at Punahou, she launched the Academy's Mandarin Chinese language program, eventually starting after-school and summer-school language programs. She chaired the Foreign Languages Department from 1986 to 1991.

Given her background as a teacher and department head, Staab was well positioned to push for new programs at the Wo International Center, expanding its reach into the Academy and the Junior School. She was particularly astute at finding ways to institutionalize the school's vision for global education, often by coordinating the educational focus of foreign exchange and international programs with long-standing Punahou values and existing curriculum objectives.

"What Hope would say is there are two things you want to give kids: empathy and multiple perspectives. That's a globally educated person," says Punahou President Jim Scott. But empathy isn't always easy to articulate to kids. Broadly speaking, empathy is about looking at situations from other points of view, enabling us to connect with and understand people who are different from ourselves. "It's about allowing yourself to experience the world through a variety of lenses so that you find yourself constantly imagining what it might be like to walk in other people's shoes," says Emily McCarren, a Spanish teacher who succeeded Staab as Wo International Center director in 2013. "This relates to critical thinking because it expands our capacity to understand situations from diverse points of view, and therefore imagine solutions or possibilities that might be out of reach if we were limited to our own perspective, range of experiences, or worldview."

Staab made an important strategic decision to change the philosophy of Punahou's student trips abroad. Since Ramler's time, students in these programs had been traveling to foreign countries, practicing their language skills, and visiting museums and landmarks. Staab broadened the learning objectives beyond language and culture. She redesigned the trips so that students got to know their host culture more intimately, prompting more purposeful introspection. She incorporated the teaching of empathy by asking students questions intended to provoke critical thinking at various stages of their travels: What were their expectations for the trip before they left? Ten days later, did those expectations change? What did their observations say about their own preconceived notions of what they'd see and feel? Asking the students to keep a journal about their experiences would enable them to see how the trip had transformed them.

Staab also introduced a community service component in an effort to make trips more personally relevant to students. Community service put students in direct contact with locals and forced them to think about the needs of the people around them. For example, she started a program with a school in Baojing, China, a rural village in Hunan province. Every other summer beginning in 2004, students visited for a month to teach English to 300 middle-school children. She also developed a partnership with EARTH (Escuela de Agricultura de la Región Tropical Húmeda) University in Costa Rica. Students traveling there study the science behind sustainability and work alongside subsistence farmers.

The students' journal entries confirm that the service-oriented trips can provoke meaningful reflection. When visiting Baojing, Thomas Lee '05 wrote that he felt irritated and unprepared when a walk to a lunch spot turned out to be a three-mile trek through rice paddies and dusty roads on a particularly hot, muggy day: "I was muttering under my breath about the heat as our shirts got soaked with sweat. I wanted to stop, but my Chinese students encouraged me with their smiles, jokes, and energy," Lee wrote. "Later on, when we had reached our checkpoint, I asked the Chinese students why none of them had complained. John, a student who later became my good friend, said that the weather was nothing compared to the other hardships they must endure, like surviving on a meager annual income of $300. It was a sobering moment, and one that I'll always remember."

In designing service-oriented trips, Staab took a careful and thoughtful approach to honoring a community's true needs. "What does service mean? Hope taught me a lot about that," says Emily McCarren. "We want to avoid the idea of poverty safaris—plowing into a village with flats of lumber and building a house that will just be used by the richest guy in town. We want to be thoughtful about the kind of impact we can have in a short amount of time, and we want to make sure it's a responsible impact."

In many ways, incorporating service into study abroad trips was a natural extension of Punahou's long-standing community service legacy. Christiane Connors '98 says a combination of study abroad and service opportunities helped propel her toward an international career. In seventh grade, she joined the Community Service Club, participating in various volunteer efforts, including cleaning taro patches. In high school, she visited Lannion, in Bretagne, France, through a Wo Center program and stayed with a host family, with whom she became close. After graduating from Georgetown University in 2002, Connors volunteered for the Peace Corps in Gabon, teaching English in a rural high school. As part of her master's degree at the University of Sussex, England, she returned to Africa for her dissertation, studying community-based responses to HIV and AIDS in Mombasa, Kenya.

Today, she combines education and service in her work in Washington, DC, where she is the director of civic engagement for the Edmund Burke School. "When I think of my own pathway, it started at Punahou," she says. "Because the opportunities were there, we responded, and that is so emblematic of Punahou. The opportunities are presented, and you can participate and then discover, 'Wow, I'm really passionate about this.'" Graduates such as Connors show that even informal service opportunities can inspire career paths, underscoring the value of building those opportunities into the curriculum.

When Staab first started retooling the Wo International Center's excursions abroad, the trips continued to be entirely separate from the academic curriculum. Participating students didn't earn any academic credits, let alone credits toward graduation. Staab and Academy Principal Kevin Conway worked together to change this. Conway was a linguist who had spent most of the 1990s living in Mexico City, teaching English at a university and later serving as the principal of the American School Foundation there; he valued the global perspective as much as Staab did. Shortly after Conway began his tenure at Punahou in 2000, the school started to grant students one-half of an elective social studies credit for several of the international trips. Staab later successfully petitioned for the Costa Rica community service trip to count for one-half of an elective science credit.

Current Wo Center Director Emily McCarren went a step further and got the administration's approval in 2013 for the school's first global CapSEEDS (Capstone in Social entrepreneurship, Economics, Environment, Deeds of service, and Sustainable solutions) course, a service-oriented trip to Senegal, to fulfill a required credit toward graduation.

Additionally, Punahou developed partnerships with schools abroad, offering semester and yearlong study abroad programs for Punahou students in China, France, and Spain, among other countries. The school also increasingly leveraged technology to create meaningful international interactions for students. It was one of ten founding schools of the Global Online Academy, an alliance that now includes more than fifty schools around the world. In the 2013–14 school year, twenty Punahou students took online classes with students from partner schools as far away as Jakarta, Indonesia, and Madaba, Jordan. Punahou faculty have taught classes for the online academy since it began in 2011.

Early on, Conway also began hiring more faculty with international teaching experience. He and Junior School Principal Mike Walker, who grew up in Mexico City, attended international school recruitment events and hired two or three teachers with international backgrounds each year, over time expanding their presence in the faculty. Conway estimates that out of 150 Academy teachers, more than 20 have worked internationally. "For our kids to be able to have people in the classroom who have lived elsewhere and experienced life elsewhere is a wonderful resource," Conway says.

Teacher trips abroad, sponsored by the Wo Center, have also become an important tool to help teachers think more globally. Every other summer since 2001, the Wo Center has been taking a group of fifteen to twenty Punahou teachers from different grade levels overseas on professional development retreats to encourage them to bring a global mindset into their classrooms. An art instructor fresh from a teacher trip to Ghana might introduce her students to traditional West African textile arts, as well as the work of contemporary Ghanaian designers, while an English teacher might introduce the work of Ghanaian poets, playwrights, and novelists.

Wo Center teacher trips and other educator programs emphasize that everyone in a school community has the opportunity and responsibility to be a global educator. In other words, global awareness is an attitude—it's about how you think.

"It's another way to look at the things we already do," says McCarren. "We're asking teachers to wonder about global education at every turn. How can I make this math lesson better by having a global mindset? Or how can I use this reading lesson to expose my kids to something that will nudge them toward more effective global citizenship?"

While the methods for teaching global concepts are constantly expanding, learning a foreign language is still a core tenet. In the Academy, Conway has added more faculty to support students taking advanced language levels, with the goal of encouraging them to keep studying languages for all four years of high school. He has also upgraded Hawaiian from an elective to a formal language sequence, with four levels that count toward graduation.

The Wo International Center tries to encourage language studies at all levels. In the last fifteen years, for example, languages have become a bigger priority for the Junior School, thanks in large part to Hope Staab's efforts. One of her signature initiatives extended language and culture programs into elementary classrooms. The Wo Center took on an incubator role for this new idea in language and culture, funding an Academy teacher to visit Junior School classrooms to teach a language once a cycle. Today, children learn basic Chinese in first grade, Japanese in second, and Hawaiian in third. The sequence reflects the primary cultures and languages of Hawai'i. The Junior School has adopted it as part of the curriculum, validating the value of teaching foreign languages as part of early childhood education.

Another Wo Center program, a weekly after-school Chinese class that Staab started, blossomed in 2013 under Emily McCarren's watch into a five-day Mandarin immersion after-school program, with enrollment open to the community. Japanese and Hawaiian after-school immersion programs began in the 2014–15 school year.

Within this environment of increased global awareness, the Wo Center also supports teachers' individual efforts to bring international perspectives into their classrooms. Leah

Anderson '94 teaches her eighth graders about public policy issues through a national program called "We the People: Project Citizen," which combines lessons in civics and hands-on work on real policy issues.

When Anderson wanted to add an international component to her lessons, McCarren and Chai Reddy, the Wo Center's associate director, helped her make contact with a Swedish middle school associated with Wo. Anderson's proposal found its way into the hands of a like-minded English teacher in Stockholm, Sweden, and together the two developed a curriculum. Throughout the 2012–13 school year, the classes exchanged emails and used Skype to discuss and develop policy proposals to address global warming.

The collaboration went so well that in the 2013 school year, the Swedish and Hawai'i teachers, with the Wo Center's help, organized an exchange visit to each other's schools. For two weeks in October, twenty-one Swedish students and three of their teachers stayed with Punahou families. They attended classes and participated in school activities. In their off hours, they went to the beach and played tourist with their host families. The following March, sixteen Punahou students went to Stockholm for spring break.

Anderson's students wrote journal entries showing the perspective they had gained through traveling and interacting with their Swedish counterparts. "To go to a school and live in a family with a different background on the other side of the Earth is honestly surreal to us, and something most of us couldn't have imagined happening before it did," the students wrote in a group reflection. "Not only did it give us the opportunity to be more independent, but we also got the chance to connect and discuss similarities and differences, and let us realize that we aren't that different after all and that we all have similar goals and ambitions, both for ourselves and society, despite the geographical gap between us."

Anderson feels it's imperative to introduce students at an early age to international perspectives. "We've got issues going on globally that can only be addressed through international collaboration," she says. "Teaching these kids at such a young age that that's possible will help them in the future—when they become the problem solvers."

One way that Punahou has introduced children as young as kindergartners to global concepts is through the *Hōkūle'a*, a Hawaiian double-hulled voyaging canoe that is navigating the Pacific on a mission to visit twenty-six countries over five years, raising awareness of global issues and sustainability. Every grade level at Punahou is learning about the voyage.

The kindergartners learned about the life cycle of the banana when they harvested the fruit from their garden to make dehydrated banana chips. The students then presented the chips to the crew of the *Hōkūleʻa*. An eighth-grade class learned about the physics of sailing and how global wind patterns will affect the canoe's progress.

In May 2014, a group of students participated in a live video chat with several crewmembers, including master navigator Nainoa Thompson '72, as they prepared for their departure from Hilo. The students asked questions about the kinds of food the crew packed for its journey and what they do when they're out at sea for longer than anticipated. Thompson's answer touched on sustainability and resource conservation.

"We have procedures to deal with being at sea longer than normal. But it means rationing, using less and less resources over time," Thompson says. "We cut the amount of food we normally eat in a day in half, so we can stretch what we have. But the big issue is water. We catch rain off the sails and we cut the water we drink in half until we get back into good winds."

Teachers asked students who were not present for the conversation with Thompson to contemplate these types of questions. One lesson—about how to pack the bare necessities for such a voyage—provoked students to reflect on what it means to live with finite resources, whether on a canoe, on an island, or on the Earth itself.

Before the *Hōkūleʻa* left Oʻahu and began its voyage in 2014, Malia Ane '72, the director of K–12 Hawaiian Studies, took busloads of Punahou teachers and students down to the dry dock to touch the canoe. Every Junior School student visited the canoe, as did many Academy students. Ane believes the first step in helping kids appreciate other cultures is for them to understand their own. Without a sense of personal history, she says, kids lack the context to frame thoughtful questions. For example, helping third graders understand that Hawaiʻi relies on ships to transport the majority of the food they eat can frame questions about food sustainability in other places on the planet.

The Wo International Center also coordinated a student trip for Academy students to Rapa Nui and Tahiti that coincided with the *Hōkūleʻa*'s landing there. Punahou hoped that, as with the canoe's mission, the Wo trip would help students develop a stronger understanding of the connection between all Polynesian peoples, despite the thousands of miles of ocean that separate them. Together, the students and community members in Rapa Nui examined issues that Hawaiʻi and Rapa Nui have in common, including the responsible growth of tourism, sustainability, and balancing cultural protection with development.

"We are trying to ensure that our programs emphasize connecting people to people, and not just people to places," says Emily McCarren. "Building on our deep sense of place at Punahou, we want our students to learn about other places through the points of view and from the perspectives of the people who call the places home."

While the gift from the Wo and Luke families focused on expanding Punahou's international programs, the Wo International Center has also sought to fulfill the school's broader mission of acting as a resource for the community. The Pan Pacific Program, which Siegfried Ramler started in 1969, has been open to students from other Hawaiʻi schools since its founding. Hope Staab made sure that all of the center's study abroad trips and programs would also be open to enrollment by non-Punahou students, as are Punahou's after-school language immersion classes.

"Punahou is a great example of a private school that has a public purpose. It does try to serve both public schools and the community," says Jill Takasaki Canfield, the executive director of the Pacific and Asian Affairs Council, a longtime Punahou partner in the community. Since 2001, the council has sponsored thirty-one students from other Hawaiʻi high schools to join Wo Center trips. "Our students come back empowered and with a sense of responsibility as global citizens. They're not only aware but also feel capable of creating positive change in the world," Canfield says.

While Staab spent many years nurturing internal relationships between the Wo Center and the rest of the school, she also worked on teacher development programs that earned the center a reputation as a place for educators to come and learn. She sought grants from the Freeman Foundation and others to develop teacher training institutes that served not only Punahou teachers but also educators from Asia, the continental United States, and elsewhere in Hawaiʻi.

For nine years, beginning in 2002, the Wo Center hosted winter and summer teacher training institutes that brought more than 300 teachers from China to Hawaiʻi to brainstorm about education issues. One year, for example, the teachers discussed early childhood learning and highlighted the differences in how Chinese and American schools approach the topic. For four years, beginning in 2006, Staab also organized summer institutes, accommodating a total of eighty-six teachers from Hawaiʻi's Department of Education, that tied global education to department benchmarks. In 2011, the National Association of Independent Schools honored Staab with its Global Citizen Award for her contributions to global education. She was the first recipient who was not a headmaster or principal.

More than forty-five years after Punahou hosted its first international students from the Keio Schools in Japan, Punahou today sends students abroad to China, Costa Rica, France, India, Italy, Japan, Jordan, Rapa Nui, Senegal, Singapore, Sweden, and Tahiti, either for study abroad during the school year or for summer service trips. The success of the study abroad trips and the teacher training institutes has positioned Punahou as a leading figure in global education. McCarren and Conway say they receive requests almost every day from schools seeking help in developing their own international trips and programs.

A highlight of the center's recent innovations is the Student Global Leadership Institute (SGLI), an intensive yearlong program that brings together about eighty students from twenty-five schools in nine countries to work together on global issues. Hope Staab and Chai Reddy, now the Wo Center's associate director, launched SGLI in 2010 in response to a challenge from the Edward E. Ford Foundation, whose charitable mission includes supporting educational initiatives. SGLI's goal is to develop an international community of young leaders who understand shared global challenges and are motivated to create positive social change. Program themes in past years have included food, health, energy, and water security and sustainability, with students developing a social action project for their home cities. After a two-week summit at Punahou, the students return to their native countries and implement their projects during their senior year, sharing their progress with fellow SGLI graduates online.

Like Staab and Ramler before them, McCarren and Reddy are continuing to develop partnerships that break new ground for the Wo International Center. In 2013, Punahou sent fifteen rising seniors to Senegal. The trip was part of the school's first global CapSEEDS course, a redesigned senior economics and community service requirement that teaches economic principles through case studies and community service. The Senegal trip required students to adapt their ideas about community service to reflect the needs of the local people.

Leigh Johnston '14, who went on the trip, says a big moment for her came when she realized that her ideas for creating lasting change did not line up with the community's own priorities. "Everybody had this idea that we needed to go and help them and make a big difference," she says. "I had to change that mentality. It was condescending to think that I was going to go in there and change people's lives in just three weeks. So when we got there, we tried to focus on what they wanted to do." In the end, the Punahou and Senegalese students put on a sustainability fair together and planted trees outside the town's hospital. The trip was one of Punahou's most audacious international endeavors to date. Going beyond familiar destinations in Asia

and Europe, McCarren and Reddy connected with a partner school that was not an established international school but instead a tiny start-up with limited resources.

What does the next frontier for global education at Punahou look like? Jim Scott's vision is for every Punahou student to have an international experience. "One of the things I would love—it probably won't happen on my watch—[would be to] have three weeks in a different culture as a requirement for graduation. I'd like to be able to fund it, so that if you can't pay that extra cost, there'd be financial aid," he says.

He wants to extend the same offer to Punahou's teachers. "I'd love to say to every teacher, 'Sometime in the next five years, you need an overseas experience, and whatever it's going to cost you, we're going to figure out a way for you to do this, because it's important for you to be thinking globally about your classroom,'" he says.

McCarren and the Wo Center are also expanding teacher training opportunities for both Punahou teachers and educators throughout the Hawai'i community, creating a kind of graduate school for teaching. "It makes a school in the middle of the Pacific seem very connected to the world when our faculty and faculty from other places feel like they're colleagues, working together on real educational issues," she says. New programs often evolve out of existing ones, such as the teacher training track that runs parallel to SGLI and serves the educators who accompany their students to Hawai'i for the institute.

Conway shares Scott's dream of having every Punahou student travel overseas, although Punahou's large size—about 425 in each graduating class—makes the logistics difficult. In the meantime, he hopes to see more international opportunities for students in Africa, Latin America, and the Middle East. "If we can't get every student out of the country, I hope we can find a way to at least get many, many more students to have a significant international experience," he says.

While helping Scott and Conway work toward those goals, McCarren says she also wants to see the Wo Center expand its role as a resource to the community. The challenge is to find ways to give even more students, at Punahou and beyond, access to Wo Center programs. "In fifteen years, if there are kids from public schools going to our after-school immersion programs, and we're running trips every summer that kids from Punahou and the Department of Education are both getting high-school credit for—then that looks like success to me," she says.

Looking at the depth of international program offerings at Punahou, it's clear the Wo Center has surpassed even the Wo brothers' original dream. In the past quarter century, the center has grown from an emerging vision to a fully integrated entity whose programs have become an integral part of the student and teacher experience. The center's reach has stretched far beyond the building. As the school has internalized the original challenge of equipping students for success in a more globalized world, its programs have expanded to touch both students and faculty in just about every grade level. SGLI embodies the current vision of global education at Punahou, bringing together students from diverse countries and backgrounds to develop solutions. The beauty of this concept is that cross-cultural teamwork can happen in a classroom on campus.

"We are continually asking ourselves, 'Are we doing the best we can to realize our mission and vision?'" says Emily McCarren. "Part of Punahou's mission is to create environments where students can appreciate cultural diversity and develop social responsibility. This is exactly the multiple perspectives and empathy that Hope always emphasized, and those things are central to a high-quality education. Wo Center remains a critical element of the school as we challenge ourselves to live up to our ambitions," she says. "We have come a long way, but there is still so much more we can do."

VANESSA ADAMS 1988

BY SARA LIN '99

Most Westerners arriving at a new job in Africa meet an office staffer and a private car at the airport. Vanessa Adams '88 showed up at her new office in Ghana in a bush taxi she took from the Togo border, having spent three hours crowded into the shared-ride vehicle with other locals.

"Usually expats come with 7,000 pounds of cargo, but here's Vanessa stepping out of a taxi with a single suitcase," says Joyjit Deb Roy, her direct supervisor and colleague of ten years. "Everyone looked at each other and said, 'Who *is* this woman?' She's not dependent on anybody. She's got that independent spirit."

Adams has never been one to wait around for things to happen. At Punahou, she took almost all advanced placement classes as a junior, and by the fall of senior year, she had enough credits to graduate a semester early. She skipped commencement in 1988 and instead enrolled in a leadership training program in Colorado.

"It's not that I couldn't wait to leave; I had amazing teachers at Punahou and really wonderful support. But there was such an exciting huge world out there," Adams says. After attending college in France, Adams founded a nonprofit focused on art and culture, helping French elementary schools

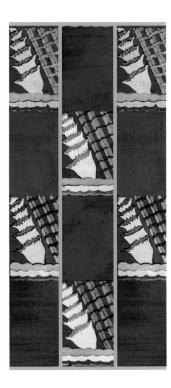

opposite
Vanessa Adams's expertise in agribusiness development supports farming enterprises, including this women-run coffee-seedling nursery located in Beko, Ethiopia.

and other community groups put on theatrical and musical productions at historical sites. She returned to the United States in 1995 and worked for a private company in Boulder, Colorado, handling operations, managing marketing initiatives, and formulating business development strategies

for US-based Fortune 500 companies in many different industries. By 2002, she was anxious to go abroad again. She joined the Peace Corps in Mali, and within two years Carana Corporation hired her under subcontract with the US Agency for International Development (USAID) to help run its West Africa Trade Hub in Ghana.

Today, Adams works for the Agricultural Cooperative Development International and Volunteers in Overseas Cooperative Assistance (ACDI/VOCA), a nonprofit that contracts with USAID, as director of its Ethiopia program, which assists 1.5 million small farmers. Put simply, her job is to help the farmers improve their livelihoods with training and business development, among other services. She also introduces the farmers to improved seed varieties, new machines, and efficient warehousing practices. The farmers need her help, but they don't have the money to pay for the services, so the US government subsidizes the program.

Still, Africa is a hard place to do business, and it takes a lot of grit to make things happen. Transporting goods overland is a costly endeavor, plagued with bribes and delays. Many farmers lack even basic knowledge about the best practices required to ensure the highest crop yield and quality. Fighting the status quo is a daily struggle.

"I'm determined to see things actually change in fundamental ways and to make a difference that matters," Adams says. "Even here, there are many development projects that are happy to just do the minimum, and I'm not. I make people crazy because I'm so insistent on doing things well and doing things at an international standard."

Her bosses describe her as a gem. In the last two and a half years, she has facilitated more than $92 million in exports. "Vanessa is by far one of the premier deal makers I've ever encountered," says Bill Polidoro, president and CEO of ACDI/VOCA, which operates in about 40 countries. "She's got an instinct, an innate understanding of the market. It's what sets her apart."

In Ethiopia, Adams works on honey, coffee, sesame, corn, wheat, and chickpeas, but coffee has the most international visibility. It's Ethiopia's biggest export at 180,000 tons, valued at $800 million a year. At an April 2014 specialty coffee convention in Seattle, Washington, Adams managed a delegation of 20 Ethiopian coffee exporters and growers. Constantly in motion, she organized everything from booth setup to meetings with major American clients including Starbucks and Costco.

The main event for the delegation was a series of sold-out cupping (tasting) sessions. Prospective buyers crowded around a long table lined with cups containing more than two dozen different kinds of dry coffee grounds. After the buyers smelled the dry grounds, baristas poured boiling water into the cups and everyone shuffled around the table, sampling a spoonful of each type. With a large slurping sound, they sucked the liquid into their mouths and then quickly spit it out into a paper cup.

Fikadu Dugassa, who represents a farmers' cooperative union covering 21,000 households in the western part of Ethiopia, was one of those who came with Adams to Seattle. He has nothing but praise for the work she has done. "She's a good person," says Dugassa, whose parents are coffee farmers. "She is the very person we need right now to understand farmers and help them overcome their problems, whether it's producing coffee of better quality or improving traceability."

Still, as a woman working in a male-dominated country such as Ethiopia, she's met her share of detractors. At a convention luncheon, she pointed to a coffee grower across the table who had bad-mouthed her when she first started. Her reaction was to do the opposite of what most people would do: She funded his project. By doing so, she made him accountable for meeting production targets and helped him work through problems, proving in the process that her strategy and direction worked. Now he's one of her biggest fans, she says. To help Ethiopian women overcome similar struggles, Adams has started the Women in Agribusiness Leadership Network to raise women's visibility in agribusiness through mentorship. The World Bank is keeping an eye on the initiative.

Adams hasn't been back to Hawai'i for a decade, but she thinks of it often. The westernmost coast of Ghana looks just like Waimānalo, she says, with coconut trees, beaches, and banyan-like trees. She described pineapple fields there that planters have sown with the same variety of Hawaiian pineapple Dole developed on O'ahu.

Adams met her husband, Emmanuel, a French national, in Mali, and together they have two children: Makena, who is seven, and Elsa, who is four. Adams is happy in Africa, but at the same time, she'd love to have her kids spend some time in Hawai'i. She says, "If you can find me the right thing to do, I'll be back in a minute."

The Winged O, the symbol for Punahou athletics featured on the gates of the Asa Thurston Physical Education Center, dates to 1919 when the school was called Oahu College. The symbol first appears in the 1919 Oahuan, the school yearbook, on the uniforms of the boys' track and field teams.

The Center houses a multi-purpose gym, six racquetball courts, a loft gym with weight-training equipment, an Academy classroom, shower and locker facilities, campus Health Center, athletic and PE department offices, and JROTC headquarters. Opened in 1981, the Center was built with a gift from Punahou School trustee Thurston Twigg-Smith '38 and his brother, David '42 in memory of their great-great-grandfather.

The athletic facilities at Punahou support more than 120 teams in 21 different sports at the inter-mediate, junior varsity, and varsity levels.

The Christopher B. Hemmeter Fieldhouse is named for Chris Hemmeter, a school trustee from 1979 to 1991, who donated funds to build a state-of-the-art gymnasium. Opened in 1981, the multi-purpose Fieldhouse was designed for basketball, volleyball, and wrestling activities, PE classes, student assemblies, and annual showcases such as May Day and Holokū.

overleaf

Alexander Field debuted in 1908 as the islands' premiere athletic field, hosting many of O'ahu's early interscholastic football games. The field is named in memory of Samuel T. Alexander (1842–60), brother of Punahou President W. D. Alexander (1849) and co-founder of Alexander & Baldwin. Construction was facilitated by a gift from Samuel Alexander's wife, Martha Cooke (1849–60) Alexander, who also provided a maintenance endowment. Punahou's Centennial pageant took place on the field on June 24–25, 1941, attracting an audience of 11,000 people over the two days. PE classes, the Punahou marching band, and other student activities continue to keep the field in constant use.

In 1982, Alexander Field underwent major renovations to add viewing stands and install an all-weather surface on the eight-lane Atherton Track, named for a lead gift from the Atherton Family Foundation.

CARISSA MOORE 2010

BY MINDY PENNYBACKER '70

A tall, broad-shouldered young woman in a purple sundress leapt across the hot asphalt fronting a food truck on Monsarrat Avenue. It was mid-June, and her light-hearted smile as she waved and called to friends expressed pure summer joy. Carissa Moore '10, had just returned home from the Brazil contest in the Association of Professional Surfing women's world championship tour.

A father and his preteen daughter approached, the girl hanging back shyly. "Carissa, could you sign my daughter's magazine?" the father asked. "Oh, sure, of course, I'd be happy to!" said Moore, with such a kind, friendly manner that the girl looked up with a big smile.

Despite Moore's unassuming air, she is a high-wattage, charismatic star. She combines island-style graciousness with the poise of an international traveler and world-class athlete.

Long before Moore became the youngest-ever Association of Surfing Professionals women's world champion—winning the title in 2011 at eighteen, then again in 2013 and 2015—everybody was talking about the part-Hawaiian girl from Honolulu who was shredding Kewalo and other breaks from the South to the North Shores. Quick, powerful, creative, and cool, she mastered all the maneuvers:

off-the-lips, multiple cutbacks, aerials, spins. "I remember seeing this little seven-year-old grom on an inside wave at Waikīkī, screaming to her dad, 'I did it!' It was Carissa—she had just completed her first 360 and she was totally stoked," remembers Marion Lyman-Mersereau '70, herself an accomplished surfer and paddler.

Soon, Moore was getting barreled. Until her generation came along, it was rare to see women score tube rides, especially in contests, which sent them out in smaller waves than those reserved for the men. "Carissa's awesome. She surfs like a boy," declared male surfers young and old, claiming her proudly as one of their own.

Sorry, guys. Moore surfs like a girl. Unlike most men, she doesn't shred for the sake of shredding and dominating, but follows the shape and flow of the wave—respecting it in classic Hawaiian style. And she's renewing and expanding the concept of what a woman can do.

In 2011, when lack of sponsorship forced cancellation of the women's Vans Triple Crown of

opposite

Carissa Moore photographed at her home in Pālolo Valley, O'ahu, in 2013, the year she won her second Association of Surfing Professionals Women's World Championship

Surfing, Moore was invited to participate as the sole woman in the men's Triple Crown contests at Hale'iwa and Sunset Beach. She took it on—she's been surfing against guys all her life. "Carissa competes with boys, not because she wants to outdo them but because she wants to learn from them," says Ruth Fletcher, who was a college counseling dean of the Punahou Class of 2010. "That's who she is, and it's rare."

Moore was one of twenty-four seniors who received the annual President's Award in 2010. "It was one of my greatest highlights ever!" Moore says. "To be recognized for something outside of surfing was so special." The award goes to students who have performed to the best of their ability academically, and who have demonstrated both leadership and teamwork—the individuals "who serve, and who give continually of themselves to others, to the school, and to living in general."

Many of Moore's classmates speak of her as the most inspiring person they knew at Punahou. Says Fletcher, Moore was "so genuine, so very humble, always positive with those around her, with this great work ethic: a great asset in all her classes. She is so comfortable in her own skin. And for a teenager that was remarkable."

Moore also demonstrated a strong sense of discipline, getting up at 5 a.m. to surf before school, and making sure she completed work for classes she missed due to surf competitions. "Surfing taught her to focus, to think strategically, to manage her time—and she brought these skills to the classroom," Fletcher adds. Because she pushed the limits in surfing, Moore wasn't afraid of tackling difficult problems and making mistakes along the way to a solution.

Many President's Award winners are leaders in extracurricular activities, from community service to sports. Moore's surfing schedule didn't permit her to participate in organized Punahou class leadership opportunities, but she led in other ways. Passionate about the ʻāina, Moore studied environmental science and took action to support her beliefs—working with a turtle release program and creating an environmental awareness section on her website called "Make a Difference."

"Carissa formed a healthy living club. About eighty people would come and surf with her and her friends on Saturdays. It wasn't a school-sanctioned club, more word of mouth, sharing their joy in the outdoors," Fletcher says.

Today, Moore volunteers with the nonprofit AccesSurf, helping people with disabilities enjoy the ocean. While she was home in May, she par-

The Buff and Blue 1901

ticipated in a fundraising event for a classmate who needed money for his kidney surgery.

During her senior year, Moore made the tough decision not to apply to college. To fulfill her potential in a fast-changing, highly physical, and acrobatic sport, she had to hit the pro circuit. "I'd love to go back to school at some point," she says. But for now, her goal is "to continue doing competitive surfing and traveling the world as long as I can." Eventually, she wants to get married, have a family, and perhaps teach environmental science to kids.

How did Punahou shape who she has become? "Punahou did a good job of supporting the individual journey," she says. "Whether you were talented in music or art or athletics, teachers helped us excel at whatever we wanted to. Being surrounded by such talented people made me want

to do my best." First and foremost, however, she credits her family. "That mentality of enjoying the whole journey—it's not about winning, it's about the experience—comes from my family, especially my dad." Moore also acknowledges the debt she owes to previous women wave riders for her opportunities and success.

That energy flows both ways: Moore inspires older women surfers, such as Lyman-Mersereau. Someday she would like to write a book for young girls. "I want to inspire girls to embrace who they are and not worry so much about what other people think. Live your life and be happy and enjoy the simple dreams."

Moore leads by example: ever generous and thankful to her fellow competitors, as well as friends, family, and others she happens to meet in life's ever-changing lineup.

INVENTING THE FUTURE

YONG ZHAO

with Academy students ⌣

MADELINE BOYLE '16

HANNAH BRODERICK '14

AVERY FARM '17

JENNIFER HA '14

CLARISSA HEART '16

KATHY LAU '14

CARTER NAKAMOTO '14

NIKKI YEE '15

BRANDON ZUNIN '15

opposite

The Omidyar K–1 Neighborhood opened in 2010, welcoming 300 kindergarten and first-grade students to an environment built for innovative teaching and learning. The planning process actively involved teachers, who brought forth the latest brain research on and teaching methods for how children best learn.

The complex is named for eBay founder and Punahou School trustee Pierre Omidyar '84 and his wife, Pam. The Omidyars provided the lead gift for the project, which was designed by UrbanWorks.

On a cold day in December 2013, in a Beijing auditorium packed with Chinese education leaders, Punahou School President Jim Scott told the proud story of his 172-year-old school. Images of Punahou's sunny campus and historic buildings made of Hawaiian basalt impressed the audience, but the educators were most interested in learning the "secrets" of the school that had produced two world leaders. Many Chinese people know Punahou as the school that educated both Dr. Sun Yat-sen, who ended China's imperial rule and founded the Republic of China more than 100 years ago, and Barack Obama, America's first African-American president.

Scott's presentation was part of "Building Schools of the Future," a forum hosted by Beijing Academy on behalf of the Chaoyang Education Commission, which manages the educational institutions for nearly 4 million people in one of Beijing's districts. China's quest for globally competent creative talents prompted the commission to develop Beijing Academy, a new pre-K to grade 12 school that will serve as a model of educational transformation and a platform for sharing innovative practices nationwide. To ensure that current best practices would inform Beijing Academy's development, the commission recruited a twelve-member International Advisory Council composed of the world's top researchers, along with leaders of schools widely recognized for their innovation. Jim Scott and California's High Tech High founder, Larry Rosenstock, were the council's two members representing K–12 schools in the United States.

The choice of Punahou as a model for the future may seem counterintuitive, given that the school was founded nearly two centuries ago. A long-standing history of accomplishment can be a powerful deterrent to change. By definition, change disrupts past practices, often in the pursuit of improvement. Therefore, institutions steeped in tradition are generally not ideal candidates for inventing the future—unless change and innovation have been integral and dynamic aspects of their history, as is the case with Punahou.

The diverse accomplishments of its alumni and students exemplify Punahou's history of excellence. Alumni include Prince Jonah Kūhiō Kalaniana'ole (1889) of the Kingdom of Hawaii, who served as a delegate to the US House of Representatives; filmmaker Li Ling Ai '26, who produced *Kukan*, the first documentary nominated for an Academy Award; twenty-two Olympic athletes, including "Buster" Crabbe '27, Lindy Vivas '75, and Keitani Graham '98; folk musicians Dave Guard '52 and Bob Shane '52, cofounders of the Kingston Trio; eBay founder Pierre Omidyar '84; and Hawai'i Senator Brian Schatz '90.

Punahou students continue to excel by traditional measures of achievement. Ninety-nine

percent of the class of 2013 is attending four-year colleges and universities; twenty-two members of the class of 2014 qualified as National Merit Scholar semifinalists; and Punahou students have claimed numerous national awards in science, math, languages, and the arts, including seven Presidential Scholar selections in the last ten years. This level of success is the result of the school's ability to balance a tradition of excellence with a culture of renewal responsive to transformative developments in globalization, neuroscience, and technology.

How is the world changing? And how do we best prepare our students for that changing world? In response to these two questions, Punahou has articulated the essential qualities that students will need in the twenty-first century: vision, optimism, creative problem solving, technological competence, global perspective, adaptability, persistence, risk taking, confidence, empathy, and cross-cultural competence. The school promotes an educational paradigm that emphasizes personalized education, project-based learning, the development of both cognitive and noncognitive capacities, and the design of globally connected environments responsive to the learning needs of students.

Punahou represents a model of education that strives to balance a number of paradoxical relationships: tradition versus innovation, human versus machine, local versus global, top-down versus bottom-up, and tinkering versus invention. Punahou's ability to embrace these paradoxes in a manner that invigorates its educational mission to encourage each child's highest potential is a defining feature of the school's excellence.

Thoughtful innovation that capitalizes on established strengths

To innovate, to introduce something new—people typically view this as a positive act, but innovations can be as harmful as they are beneficial. Institutions must undertake changes thoughtfully, yet without allowing caution to paralyze them. They must also calibrate the scale, speed, and timing of change to their institutional capacity. Successful organizations work hard to strike the optimal balance between maintaining tradition and embracing change. Punahou's innovations have capitalized on the school's strengths, including its history, campus, and alumni. The school's adoption of entrepreneurial education offers an illustrative example.

Since the nineteenth century, America's educational system has operated on a factory-based model, designed to produce employees who could fill well-defined jobs within traditional, top-down industries. This standardized approach to education no longer aligns with the global marketplace, as Thomas Friedman pointed out in his 2005 book, *The World Is Flat*. To succeed in the twenty-first century, students need to become entrepreneurs—individuals who possess the foresight and boldness to build something new.

K–12 schools in the United States have been slow to respond to this escalating need. Some educators view the goals of entrepreneurship—taking a product to market and reaping a profit—as antithetical to the aims of education. Defined more broadly, however, entrepreneurship is about turning ideas into action. A social entrepreneur finds inventive ways to address persistent community issues, prompting positive social change.

Turning to the history of the school, one could view Punahou's missionary founders as entrepreneurs in terms of their efforts to promote education and literacy in the islands. After arriving in 1820, they issued the first Hawaiian-language newspaper in 1834, published the Hawaiian translation of the Bible in 1839, and founded schools throughout the islands. The missionaries' tradition of creating positive social change through service continues today at Punahou through the programs of the Luke Center for Public Service. Punahou magnified its focus on service and its entrepreneurial spirit in 2006 when trustee Steve Case '76, the cofounder of America Online (AOL), launched the Daniel H. Case III '75 Social Entrepreneurship program to bring outside experts to campus. Spurred by this initiative, Punahou started the Entrepreneurs in Residence (EIR) Program two years later.

The EIR Program capitalizes on the expertise of Punahou alumni, parents, and friends by inviting entrepreneurs from Hawai'i businesses and nonprofits to mentor Academy students. Along with acquiring real-world experience, students gain insights into the value of persistence and failure. Schools typically teach students to avoid making mistakes, but "to make big impacts, you have to be willing to make mistakes," says an EIR mentor. "You have to have the will to succeed and the willingness to fail."

In 2009, incoming freshmen Cuyler Hirata '12 and Kelly Ann Lee '12 joined the EIR Program with the desire to lift the spirits of seniors living in care homes. But their initial plan to provide live musical entertainment fell flat when they realized music's short-lived effect on the seniors. Returning to the drawing board, the students came up with Plan B, and then Plan C. After two years of setbacks, the students and their EIR mentors developed a winning formula: Hirata and Lee would videotape interviews with the seniors and compile an edited DVD of each remarkable life story, which they presented to the elder and his or her family. By focusing on the seniors' strengths, the students achieved and surpassed their original purpose, illustrating how real-life consequences inspire authentic learning.

Located on the mauka end of the campus, the Omidyar K–1 Neighborhood includes twelve classrooms and their gardens encircling a large central lawn. A natural bioswale—a dry streambed or a streamlet depending on rainfall—wends its way through the complex. The K–1 curriculum focuses on our island home and the ahupua'a of Mānoa. Students explore the benefits of caring for the land, from the mountains to the sea, and the corresponding concept of the inter-relatedness of all life forms.

185

Punahou has embraced entrepreneurship across campus as a way to expand students' understanding of our interdependent world. A twelfth-grade course, CapSEEDS (Capstone in Social entrepreneurship, Economics, Environment, Deeds of service, and Sustainable solutions), engages students in addressing urgent needs in the Hawai'i community. Students in the Junior School explore entrepreneurship through hands-on projects that capitalize on their natural curiosity.

One morning in May 2014, second graders in the classrooms of Natalie Hayashi and Caryn Nakamura '90 Matsuoka bustled about, selling homemade wares as parents and faculty browsed the crowded aisles. Market Day, adapted from the Mini Society program for grades three and up, was the culmination of a yearlong interdisciplinary project that examined the core principles of the global economy.

Students began by observing where the food they consume comes from and discovered that bananas often originate in Ecuador, highlighting the global nature of trade. They learned about the financial and environmental costs of transporting food across the seas, which sparked class discussions on the importance of buying local produce to encourage food self-sufficiency in Hawai'i.

Children worked in small groups to conduct market research, which they used to fashion products targeted to needs they identified. Encouraged to make sustainable items, one team up-cycled water bottles into pencil holders, while another made whimsical toys from discarded socks. Along the way, students designed their own currency, practiced basic budgeting, and learned how to launch a business—registering for a license, building a brand, and filming commercials on their iPads.

The students' hard work paid off. On Market Day, products flew off the tables, while children practiced their fledgling math skills by calculating sales totals and returning change. Hayashi counted the experience a success. "The currency may have been invented, but the lessons they learned were very real," she said.

Educational transformation through technology ⌢

Beginning in 1994, Punahou provided its students with Internet capabilities, at a time when only 0.4 percent of the world's population (25 million people) had Internet access; today, nearly 50 percent of the world's population (over 3 billion people) has access. In 1995, when Punahou set up its own Web server, fewer than 10,000 websites existed; today, that number is approaching 200 million. The school created its website at around the same time the White House did.

In 1997, Punahou students in grades four and nine began using individual laptop computers in classes. In the 2001–02 school year, Punahou equipped all fourth graders with laptops, launching the school's one-to-one laptop program, which now spans grades four to twelve. Today the school invests about $5 million in technology each year.

Of course, that investment is not just about technology—it's also about education. Just providing equipment and connectivity is not enough. To foster digital competency for its faculty and students, a school must also encourage human ingenuity, essential to tapping modern technology's abundant educational opportunities. In their 2014 book, *The Second Machine Age*, Erik Brynjolfsson and Andrew McAfee argue that we have entered a period in which digital technology will transform society, heightening the need for creative thinking.

As an education pioneer in the Second Machine Age, Punahou understands that teachers drive educational change. "Punahou is very thoughtful and intentional about the way we use technology. We invest heavily in supporting our teachers and their learning so they're better able to foster the creativity and curiosity of our students," says Wendi Kamiya, the school's director of information technology. She points to strong professional development and dedicated curriculum resource teachers—three in the Junior School and two in the Academy—as forming the backbone of the school's technology program.

In 2012, Academy English teacher Brian Johnson decided to develop an electronic textbook for "Buddhist Philosophy and the Game of Go," a popular course he created. The semester-long elective combines the study of Eastern Buddhism and Go, one of the world's most sophisticated games of strategy, with Western poetry and philosophy. As students learn to play, they reflect on how the game's philosophical framework might help them make better ethical decisions. For example, one of the pillars of Buddhist belief is the concept of interconnectedness. Go pieces acquire value and meaning within the game through their connection to other pieces. Being mindful of this principle of interconnectedness led students to consider how their actions—in life and in the game of Go—have an impact on everything around them.

Johnson worked with curriculum resource teachers to release his e-textbook, *Beginner's Mind: An Introduction to the Game of Go*. The interactive platform, which allows students to view animated tutorials on key moves and to experiment with plays through a drag-and-drop feature, has elevated their understanding of the game. Students review the tutorials outside class, which frees class time for personalized instruction targeted to a student's level of progress. Johnson, who is now a sought-after e-textbook consultant to campus faculty, sees the project as

The ceramic-tile mosaic set within the Hawaiian Garden of the Overton Outdoor Learning Center depicts the ahupuaʻa of Mānoa as an interconnected mauka-to-makai system with the spring Kapunahou at its center. The mosaic was created by the Omidyar K–1 Neighborhood's inaugural classes during the 2010–2011 school year and was a key part of the curriculum.

Over the course of the year, children learned about the legend of Kapunahou and studied the plants and animals associated with traditional Hawaiian life in the ahupuaʻa. Working with composition, color, and clay, each child contributed to the mural. K–1 art teacher Arlene Merritt directed the year-long project, with assistance from mosaic artist Leah Kilpatrick '86 Rigg, who installed the mural.

a promising step forward in the quest to provide students with "tailor-made textbooks designed around how they learn best."

The same willingness to explore technology's potential prompted Cheryl Durso to examine how MinecraftEdu could better engage her fifth graders in English and social studies. The popular 3-D computer game has a Lego-like structure that allows children to create an immersive virtual world. After researching the game and consulting with curriculum resource teachers, Durso introduced MinecraftEdu as a supervised, supplementary exercise. For example, as the class learned about the Mayflower Compact that governed the Pilgrims' first colonies, students decided to work on their own "Minecraft Compact" to encourage cooperation and respect within the game and the classroom. Durso observed that a group that re-created the Jamestown settlement in Minecraft retained more of the historical information because the students were building to scale in three dimensions. Students relished the game experience, and many begged to stay after school to work on their team projects.

As technology becomes more ubiquitous in the classroom, teachers take on a different role. Rather than simply providing content, teachers will be guiding children's success by igniting their personal creativity, giving them choices, and providing a range of tools so they can create their own learning portfolio. Similarly, Punahou provides teachers with professional opportunities for growth and mastery that help realize technology's educational potential, including the annual Lab School at Punahou, which offers cohort-based work on curriculum design and implementation, and teaching for the Global Online Academy, a worldwide consortium of independent schools that aims to define best practices in online education. Jim Scott says he sees teachers becoming "facilitators, innovators, mentors, and partners in learning with students."

Punahou's challenge for the future will be to continue to exploit technology's promise while ensuring that all students fully develop their capacities to problem solve, empathize, communicate, imagine, and wonder.

Global engagement rooted in the local community ⁓

Globalization presents a multitude of challenges to K–12 educational institutions, which historically have been defined by their geographical location. But today's "flat world," as Thomas Friedman described it, enables people, information, and products to move rapidly across an interdependent global village. Today, K–12 schools must prepare students to work in a global society in addition to encouraging their engagement with local community.

Through the years, Punahou has developed an expansive network of partnerships with schools around the world. Beginning in the 1960s, the school invited international students to campus each summer to learn English, and sent Hawai'i youth overseas to learn French, Japanese, and Chinese. Thousands of students participated in programs involving a dozen nations and scores of partner schools in Asia, Africa, Central America, Europe, and the Pacific. After the Wo International Center opened in 1994, Punahou's global education programs accelerated both on and off campus. Today, the center continues to facilitate global engagement by offering professional development programs for educators from partner institutions worldwide, and travel experiences for teachers and students from Punahou and other Hawai'i schools that center on building cross-cultural competence through service learning.

In 2010 Punahou launched the Student Global Leadership Institute (SGLI), an annual program that builds upon its global network of partners, to inspire young leaders committed to solving complex issues such as energy scarcity and food security affecting both their home and communities abroad. SGLI mentors and presenters have included US Secretary of Energy Steven Chu and US Food and Drug Administration Commissioner Margaret Hamburg. SGLI strives to show how successful global efforts are inseparable from local issues, people, culture, and geography, and how an understanding of one's history, culture, and environment anchors a global mindset. The more engaged students are in their local community, the better they will be able to consider global issues meaningfully.

Punahou is an educational partner in the locally based global initiative known as the Worldwide Voyage to promote mālama honua, the Hawaiian concept of caring for the Earth. Through the efforts of the Honolulu-based Polynesian Voyaging Society, Punahou students learn of the legendary achievements of the ancient Hawaiians, who sailed between Hawai'i and Tahiti. In 1976, contemporary voyages conducted using ancient techniques of navigation, based on the stars and the patterns of winds and waves, reinvigorated the cultural links between Hawai'i and the far-flung islands of Polynesia, and revived pride in all aspects of Hawaiian identity. Traditional master navigator Nainoa Thompson '72 cites astronaut Lacy Veach '62 as the inspiration for today's Worldwide Voyage—navigating Polynesian voyaging canoes around the world in order to raise awareness of the environmental issues endangering our Earth. When viewing the planet from space in the early 1990s, astronaut Veach realized the importance of the Hawaiian concept of mālama honua. He told Thompson, "You can never believe the beauty of Island Earth until you see it in its entirety from space....The best place to think about the

Originally designed as a boys' dormitory by architect Charles W. Dickey, Wilcox Hall was probably inspired by both Old School Hall and the Wai'oli mission house built by Dickey's grandfather, Rev. W. P. Alexander, and later renovated by missionary teacher Abner Wilcox, who raised his family at Wai'oli. Wilcox Hall is named for his son, George Norton Wilcox (1850–60), a philanthropist, politician, and Punahou School trustee from 1882 to 1901.

The building, which opened in 1937, was funded by the G. N. Wilcox Trust and members of the Wilcox family. After the school ended its boarding program in 1963, Wilcox Hall served as home to the school's kindergarten classes for forty-five years. The building underwent a 1988 renovation by architect John Hara '57 that added a classroom annex. Today Wilcox Hall has been transformed into a center for K–1 art, music, and creative learning and contains the Neighborhood's administrative offices.

fate of our planet is right here in the islands. If we can create a model for well-being here in Hawai'i, we can make a contribution to the entire world."

Launched in 2013, the five-year voyage will visit eighty-five ports in twenty-six countries to raise awareness of mālama honua and engage with international leaders and communities. In August 2014, in Apia, Samoa, United Nations Secretary-General Ban Ki-moon and world-renowned ocean scientist Sylvia Earle joined the crews for a sail. Five faculty members from Punahou also welcomed the canoes in Apia during a cultural exchange with K–12 schools, where they taught classes on the history and techniques of traditional navigation and shared the mission of mālama honua. In 2015, teams of teachers from Punahou also traveled to New Zealand and Australia in support of the Worldwide Voyage's educational goals.

Punahou's engagement with the Worldwide Voyage involves the whole campus—the school hosts and participates in workshops with educators across the state to take advantage of the wealth of educational opportunities the project affords; classrooms are connected digitally to the canoes; and students are planting, cultivating, and harvesting food for the voyagers. A 20-by-40-foot "voyaging garden" grows taro, sweet potato, and banana, representing the foods Polynesians brought when they settled the islands. Hundreds of students tend the garden, where they learn about the Hawaiian cultural practices that supported a self-sustaining system of food cultivation. As the canoes journey around the world, teachers and alumni from Punahou will continue to carry the fruits of students' labors to the crews.

Community-driven change inspired by thoughtful leadership ⌒

How can long-standing institutions like Punahou continue to innovate? Where do good ideas come from? And how do they gain traction? Innovations tend to either be top-down, with change mandated by leadership, or bottom-up, with ideas emerging from the grassroots level. The top-down approach can be efficient and effective, provided that leadership has ultimate authority to make decisions and promotes the right ideas. But given that such conditions are rare, most top-down innovations fail. While the bottom-up approach has a greater likelihood of success, a lack of resources and insufficient scale can hobble it. To create far-reaching change, ideas need to have bold vision and the fortification of institutional support.

Punahou's innovations have combined a grassroots approach with leadership that challenges people to envision ambitious goals. "Jim recognizes good ideas," says Junior School Principal Mike Walker, whom Scott encouraged to bring the latest research in neuroscience to

Whimsical ceramic creatures perch upon a wall outside the Castle Art Center, overlooking Rice Field with Dillingham Hall in the distance. In ceramics—throwing, building, glazing, and firing—students explore the multicultural history of ceramic objects and clay as a multifaceted medium with great expressive possibilities.

The Samuel and Mary Castle Art Center, dedicated in 1979, features studios for glassblowing, ceramics, and jewelry. The open-air structure was designed by architect Ernest Hara '28 to dissipate heat generated by glassblowing and ceramics (pp. 198–199). Punahou is one of the few high schools in the nation to offer a glassblowing program, which began in 1972.

Castle Art Center enables students and faculty to work together in close proximity as they hone technical skills and become more adept with a range of materials. This studio art environment emphasizes participatory critique and promotes individual expressive capabilities.

Hawaiʻi through the school's Brain Symposium. The annual two-day conference, which is open to educators worldwide, features leading experts sharing their insights on the educational applications of neuroscientific research. Since 2010, the symposium has presented noted practitioners and researchers such as Frank Kros, David Eagleman, John Medina, Daniel Siegel, and Carol Dweck. Some of their ideas helped inform the design of the Omidyar K–1 Neighborhood, built to reflect the developmental importance of play, an arts-centered student experience, and an environment that integrates indoor and outdoor learning.

The Brain Symposium is an example of Punahou's entrepreneurial approach to ensuring that innovations are invigorating and financially sustainable. Continuous exposure to new ideas challenges faculty to think more expansively about their instructional practices, while the Brain Symposium and other professional programs are structured to be financially self-supporting. These programs also support the school's aspirations to serve the broader educational community.

"I want us to look up and look out," Jim Scott says of his vision for Punahou. The school generously supports faculty participation in conferences, and promotes their engagement with a global community of educators. Professional Programs at Punahou, launched in 2014, gives heightened support to professional development, a cornerstone of Punahou's commitment to faculty excellence. Professional Programs seeks to bridge the worlds of theory and practice by encouraging K–12 teachers to pilot instructional ideas that can spark educational change.

Students, too, are encouraged to test out ideas. The Design Thinking Club, created in the 2013–14 school year, sprang from an informal brainstorm among a group of sophomores, facilitated by a parent trained in the process. In the 1990s, Design Thinking gained popularity within business circles as a way to spur innovation; more recently, the process has taken hold at several independent schools nationwide.

The 22-member Academy club meets twice a week to immerse itself in the methodology of Design Thinking, which involves a systematic, five-step cycle of empathy, synthesis, ideation, prototyping, and storytelling. The students' expertise and enthusiasm caught the attention of teachers. A team of Punahou seventh-grade faculty worked with the club to develop a multidisciplinary, inquiry-based project on ways to restore the physical and cultural environment of Kahoʻolawe, the Hawaiian island that was used by US Armed Forces as a bombing range from World War II to 1990. Club members and teachers later shared their insights in a joint presentation to Punahou's K–12 faculty.

Club members also shared their knowledge of Design Thinking's methodology and process

with the broader community. In June 2014, the club's founders led a five-hour workshop on Maui for twenty-seven public- and private-school educators. Workshop sponsors invited the teens back to Maui for a follow-up session in the fall, and public-school teachers completing both sessions will receive two professional development credits. The Design Thinking Club at Punahou is an example of how student-led, real-world learning generates its own momentum.

Punahou also understands the importance of allowing people to experiment with ideas that may not succeed in the end. Academy Principal Kevin Conway notes that faculty and staff feel they "can fail and ditch ideas." When people are allowed to fail, they are not afraid to generate ideas. When leadership and colleagues meet new ideas with encouragement and trust, people are inspired to bring forth other ideas. When the institution supports ideas with resources, those ideas become innovative programs. Punahou has been able to attract forward-thinking people from around the world because of its generative learning community. As a result, ideas are constantly emerging, creating a school-wide tradition of innovation.

Tinkering versus invention ⌣

Tinkering toward Utopia is a seminal book by David Tyack and Larry Cuban that examines a century of reforms in American education. The authors conclude that, despite hopes for transformative reform, actual changes have been gradual and incremental. As a result, American education—and education globally—has not kept pace with dramatic shifts in the world. Tinkering with reform may not be the answer; we may need to boldly invent our way toward educational utopia.

Punahou's innovations include both tinkering and invention. The freedom to pursue both approaches has allowed the school's learning environments to absorb new insights from neuroscience and education. The Omidyar K–1 Neighborhood at Punahou, which opened in 2010 and serves 300 children in kindergarten and first grade, exemplifies the reinvention of Punahou's educational model.

The design of the Omidyar K–1 Neighborhood builds on the pioneering design of the Mary Persis Winne Elementary Units, which originally served grades one to five. Designed by renowned architect Vladimir N. Ossipoff, the units were constructed in the 1950s on the design principle of "unity of the outdoors and adaptability to progress." Notable features include the complex's site specificity, which takes advantage of north-south sunlight, the cross-ventilation of trade winds, and the seamless flow between indoor and outdoor spaces. International archi-

ELEMENTARY SCHOOL

tectural organizations hailed the Winne Units as a triumph of modern educational design, and they went on to serve students for more than six decades.

Today, our understanding of brain development and of pedagogical best practices supports a more flexible instructional model that the structure of the Winne Units doesn't easily accommodate, as they organize students by age into self-contained classrooms. To encourage each child's full potential, faculty are collaborating intentionally across classes and grade levels; they recognize the benefits of looping—having young children stay in teams for more than one year—and they embrace an arts-centered curriculum that draws on the natural environment as a classroom. Tinkering was not enough; changing times called for a reinvention of the learning environment, exemplified by the Omidyar K–1 Neighborhood.

The K–1 Neighborhood's structure gives children an extended two-year span to develop at their own pace. Each kindergarten class is paired with a first-grade class in an adjoining classroom, and students stay with their team throughout both years. This looping allows children the benefit of learning within a familiar physical and social environment; teachers also benefit from having the ability to build a two-year sequence of instruction. In kindergarten, for example, children learn about their relationship to mauka, the mountain-oriented system that involves rain cycles, freshwater streams, plants, and animals. They build on this knowledge in first grade, when their focus turns to makai and they explore how the ocean, fishes, and plants complete the natural cycle. The result of three years of highly collaborative tinkering by K–1 teachers, the study of mauka and makai encourages young children to forge important connections to their island home. When learning is recursive, hands-on, and student-centered, it creates the foundation for lifelong curiosity and confidence, says K–1 Supervisor JoAnn Wong-Kam.

Brain research confirms what early childhood educators have long known—that the arts are an important source of cognitive engagement. This is especially important for young children, whose brains are in the formative stages of growth. Studies show that involvement in the arts activates the areas of the brain responsible for abstract thinking: The more new neural pathways that fire, the more connections a child's brain makes between subjects, reinforcing comprehension. The Neighborhood features a dedicated art studio that children visit in small groups to ensure that they receive personalized instruction from the arts specialist. Each classroom also connects to an adjoining project room where children can paint, tinker, and express themselves visually. One kindergarten and first-grade team transformed their shared project room into a rainforest filled with paper trees, vines, and butterflies, created through their

exploration of painting, collage, and clay techniques. Another team created an artistic rendering of a loʻi kalo, or taro patch, in their project room, using paintings and photos the students had taken on field trips.

Brain research also guided the design of the Neighborhood's outdoor environment. Neuroscience shows that physical activity boosts brainpower by increasing the flow of oxygen to the brain and by reinforcing its molecular structure. Additionally, engaging with the complex and unpredictable natural world builds on the brain's innate ability to solve problems.

During recess, the Neighborhood's expansive central lawn teems with children playing or exploring its semi-wild areas. A favorite place for kids to play is the bioswale, a dry bed of boulders, plants, and rocks that turns into a light stream on rainy days. While playing in the bioswale, one first-grade class became intrigued by the different kinds of rocks they found. This led to an inquiry-based exploration on the uses of rocks, historic rocks on the Punahou campus, and how rocks serve useful purposes such as filtering rainwater. Through their play and inquiry, children developed a hands-on understanding of systems, natural and artificial.

While the siting and design of the K–1 classroom explore sun and wind patterns, the rooftops—covered with photovoltaic panels—reflect the Neighborhood's role as a teaching tool for energy conservation and sustainability. The PV panels generate 90–100 percent of the complex's energy needs, which children track in real time through a Web-based tool.

Punahou is not the only school to adopt a neuroscientific approach to learning or to implement looping and an arts-centered curriculum, but its teachers have woven these approaches into a cohesive whole that supports how their children learn best. Faculty members continue to both tinker and invent. "We're still evolving into what we want to be—we keep stretching," says Wong-Kam. "We want to look at more edible landscapes, we want to look at more flexible uses of time, and we want our curriculum to be more focused on children's questions."

Throughout its history, Punahou has been open to new possibilities that inspire great teaching and learning, seizing upon challenges, difficulties, and risks as opportunities for growth. In the coming years, this approach will guide the school's implementation of its Campus Master Plan for grades two to five, which envisions the learning environments of the future. Campus-wide discussions among teachers, administrators, students, and staff have raised timely and provocative questions that have included the role of the library, the need for open space, the balance between historic and contemporary structures, the evolution of resource-efficient, environmentally responsible building practices, and the need for flexible spaces that encourage creativity and collaboration among and between students and faculty. How Punahou navigates these complex questions will be as illuminating as the answers themselves.

Jim Scott often speaks of the generative power that comes from "holding the tension" between paradoxical forces, and the school's successes indicate that students, faculty, and staff at Punahou have learned to thrive upon paradox and change as springboards for educational growth. Our ever-changing world is full of uncertainty and contradictions, and Punahou continues to embrace these with confidence and creativity. This is the real secret of Punahou's long-standing success.

This interisland flight in a biplane is one of the featured illustrations in the book Kimo: The Whistling Boy, published in 1928 by Alice Cooper (1907) Bailey and illustrated by Lucille Holling. Set in Hawai'i in the early years of the Territory of Hawaii, the book is one in a series by Bailey of historical fiction books for children. Bailey's father, attorney Henry E. Cooper, held posts in the governments of the Republic of Hawaii and the Territory of Hawaii. A copy of the book is in the collection of Cooke Library.

BYRON WASHOM 1967

BY SARA LIN '99

At his Punahou School admission interview, all Byron Washom '67 talked about was how much he loved surfing. His mom almost fainted when she heard that, but Washom, who was 13 at the time, derived an important lesson from the experience. "What I learned was, if you're passionate about what you believe in or what really drives you, there will be a place that welcomes you," he says.

Washom credits Tom Metcalf, who was then class dean, with seeing him as a diamond in the rough. He was more an explorer than a bookworm, almost flunking physics and getting a C in algebra. Yet Punahou was "a springboard to life," Washom says. "It groomed me and polished me."

Years later, a US Department of Energy program manager detected the same unbridled passion that Punahou had seen and funded Washom's proposal for a solar project, even though he had unabashedly put in a bid four times higher than what the department had budgeted. The company Washom founded with the award funds, Advanco Corporation, set eight world records in 1984 for the conversion of sunlight to electricity, including one for best conversion efficiency that stood for 24 years.

Today, the renewable energy industry regards Washom as one of its leading minds. At the Uni-

As an adventurous boy on Midway, Byron Washom experienced the challenges of living on an island with extremely limited resources.

versity of California, San Diego, where he is the director of strategic energy initiatives, he helped develop one of the largest microgrids in the country. Microgrids enable small groups of buildings to generate and store enough power so that they can isolate themselves and keep power flowing in an emergency. The idea has gained a lot of attention in recent years as a way to make local grids more resilient during major storms and other disasters. Lauded as one of the nation's most successful experiments in sustainability, the UC San Diego

microgrid meets 92 percent of the electricity needs for the 48,000-student campus over the course of a year—and it does so for half of what it would cost to buy that energy through traditional channels.

Washom calls UC San Diego's microgrid "the art of the possible," and he has demonstrated that it is not just a one-off experiment but a sustainable model that will function in other places. His team helped successfully replicate the project twice: once at University of Hawai'i Maui College, with an array one-tenth the size of UC San Diego's, and a second time on Marine Corps Base Camp Pendleton, with a microgrid four times the size of the original. His work so impressed billionaire Larry Ellison that he tapped Washom to lead his efforts to develop Lāna'i into a cutting-edge sustainable energy showpiece.

"Deep down he's a person of tremendous heart," says Chaz Feinstein, the World Bank's sector manager for water and energy for East Asia and the Pacific. He and Washom have collaborated many times over the last two decades.

"There's almost a missionary zeal to him," Chaz adds. "This is a man who, fairly early in his career, made it in life in terms of financial success. Yet he wakes up every day working as hard as he did as a struggling engineer."

Washom, who has a calm baritone voice, says he focuses on renewable energy because of its potential impact in developing countries. If he can develop successful sustainable systems, children in rural areas will have light to read by at night. A steady electricity source also means mothers who typically spend hours harvesting firewood for cooking can instead spend the time more productively, parenting or doing other work.

Washom's experiences as a little boy shaped his interest in sustainability. When he was eight, he moved to Midway Atoll, where his father served as a naval supply officer, for a year and a half. The island had a population of 400 and virtually no natural resources, meaning that supplies came in by boat once a month and everyone had to conserve.

Midway is also where Washom learned to be competitive. He would wake at dawn and rush to the beach to be the first to collect the glass balls that had washed ashore from Japanese fishing nets. He was so efficient at it that other families asked his parents to keep him in bed longer so their children could collect some glass balls, too.

On Lāna'i, Washom has found another sponsor who sees his passion and wants him to push past every limit with a renewable energy infrastructure that utilizes the sun, wind, and ocean. Though Washom is not giving away the details—Larry Ellison plays his cards close to the chest, he says—he calls it a "Herculean effort," grounded in his work at UC San Diego.

It's fitting that after four decades of living in the continental United States, Washom's work has led him back to Hawai'i. "It's my kuleana," he says. "It's a perfect word to describe both the obligation and privilege to be bringing back home what I've learned."

As chairman and CEO of Revolution LLC, a Washington, DC-based investment firm he co-founded in 2005, Steve Case partners with visionary entrepreneurs to create significant "built to last" new businesses.

right
The Case Middle School complex for sixth, seventh, and eighth graders is named for Daniel H. '42 and Carol Holmes Case. Dan served as a Punahou trustee from 1970 to 2000, and Carol taught in the Junior School and served as an Academy college counselor. They are shown here at Malaekahana, O'ahu, just after their engagement in 1954.

STEVE CASE 1976

BY JULIA FLYNN SILER

Stephen M. Case '76 gestures toward the wooden reception desk in his Washington, DC, offices. "It's koa," he explains, referring to the *Acacia koa*, one of Hawai'i's native trees, which produces a highly prized hardwood. Case's choice of this wood, with its warm reddish tones, is just one of the ways he stays in touch with Hawai'i, the place he considers his home.

A more significant way he has stayed connected is through his commitment to Punahou School. He has served as a trustee of the school since 2003, and he and his family provided a catalytic gift toward the design and building of Case Middle School, a project aimed at transforming the way adolescents learn, completed in 2004. Strong ties to Punahou run in the family. His father, Daniel H. Case '42, served as a trustee for three decades, from 1970 to 2000, and his mother Carol taught elementary school and then was a college counselor through his years there. All three of Steve's siblings, Carin '75, Jeff '80, and Dan '75 (who died of a brain tumor in 2002), graduated from Punahou. "Punahou was imprinted on me when I was born," he explains. "I grew up with it as the backdrop to my childhood."

One of America's best-known entrepreneurs, Case is now the chairman of the Startup America

Partnership, a bipartisan national effort to show how entrepreneurial thinking can power change. Born and raised in Honolulu, he is a member of the school's Thirteen Year + club and attended Punahou from kindergarten through twelfth grade. "My parents were always deeply loyal to the school," he recalls, so much so that they told him

and his siblings not to expect an inheritance from them because they planned to leave all their money to the school when they died. Whether that helps explain Case's early entrepreneurial ventures—including stocking the vending machines at the Punahou tennis courts and selling greeting cards and newspaper subscriptions door-to-door—is unclear, but from an early age, he was intent on learning as much as he could about business.

Later on, as a high school junior, he joined his classmates in organizing that year's Punahou Carnival. His job was to organize and run twenty to thirty game booths, making sure that each was fully staffed and running smoothly. As the news editor of *Ka Punahou*, the high school newspaper, he displayed early enterprise by grabbing the opportunity to cover concerts by Elton John and Jefferson Starship when these big-name rock stars came to Honolulu. His yearbook page includes his prized ticket stub from the press section seat for the heavy metal band Aerosmith. The quote he chose for his yearbook page—"Climb high, Climb far, Your goal the sky, Your aim the star"—is the inscription on Hopkins Gate at Williams College, where he would soon be heading.

Case graduated from Punahou in 1976 and then left Hawai'i for college at Williams, majoring in

At the Case family home in Mānoa, c. 1973: (from left) Carin H. '75, Stephen M. '76, parents Carol H. and Daniel H. '42, Jeffrey H. '80, and Daniel H. III '75.

political science. He worked as a pizza marketer in one of his first jobs after college. Case then went on to cofound America Online (now known as AOL Inc.) and played a key role in its $165 billion merger with Time Warner in 2001, which at the time was the single largest merger in US corporate history. That merger ultimately failed, but Case went on to set up the Case Foundation, of which he is the chairman, overseeing its philanthropic projects with his wife, Jean. He also formed an investment company called Revolution, which has backed start-ups such as Zipcar and LivingSocial. Recently, he has been leading a White House entrepreneurship campaign aimed at encouraging

US firms to invest in small businesses, including those in Hawai'i. He's one of America's highest-profile entrepreneurs, with over 759,000 followers on Twitter. In 2014, Case returned to Punahou over Carnival weekend, visiting his brother Jeff and his two nephews, Will '21 and Sam '21 Case, who both currently attend the school. The highlight for Case was taking his nephews on some of the rides. "Technology may have advanced in the last few years, but bumper cars are still bumper cars and malasadas are still malasadas."

Members of the class of 2014 raise
their voices in song during Baccalaureate.
For more than a hundred years, Punahou
baccalaureate services have been held
at Central Union Church, beginning when
the church was located on the corner
of Beretania and Richards Streets.

In recent years, graduating classes have
sung "Ho'onani Ka Makua Mau," the
English doxology translated into Hawaiian
by Rev. Hiram Bingham; the "Queen's
Prayer," a song composed in 1895 by
Queen Lili'uokalani asking the Lord's
forgiveness of those who had wronged
her; and "Hawai'i Aloha," a nineteenth-
century hymn, lyrics by Rev. Lorenzo Lyons,
that is significant today as an expression
of aloha 'āina—love for the land and
the islands of Hawai'i.

President W. D. Alexander retired from
Punahou in 1871 to become surveyor
general of the Hawaiian Kingdom.
At the end of that school-year term,
he addessed the students, "I shall know
you henceforth no longer as my pupils,
but simply as my friends.... I shall
watch your career through life with
deep interest, and with pride, I hope."

Thirty-four years later, his student
Emma Metcalf (1852–1865) Beckley
Nakuina wrote, "Long after I left school,
and he was no longer a teacher at
Punahou, and I a gray-haired mother
and grandmother, I went confidently
and freely to him (sure of his patient,
kindly help) for the elucidation or en-
lightenment on the many problems
I felt he could solve better than anyone
else. I loved and respected him next
to my father, and he was always in
my mind, the dear old 'Prof' of
my school days."

215

JOHN LEONG 1996
JULIANNA RAPU LEONG 1997

BY JULIA STEELE

In the fall of 1995, John Leong '96 was a senior at Punahou when he walked into Cooke Library and, as he remembers it, saw a beautiful young woman. Julianna Rapu '97 was a junior and a recent immigrant from Rapa Nui, the famed East Polynesian island of the moai. John was an Oʻahu boy—his grandfather started Waikīkī's Wailana Coffee House—but the two became fast friends when they found they had much in common: a love for the outdoors, an appreciation for the simple things in life, and a sense of responsibility for the wider world. They started dating the summer after John graduated and stayed together throughout their time in college, undeterred by the fact that they were on opposite coasts: John at the Wharton School, University of Pennsylvania, and Julianna at Scripps College in California.

Their college experiences only heightened their sense of what they truly valued. Julianna, living on a continent for the first time, found herself yearning for islands and inspired by her grandmother to live a life of service. An ever-resourceful woman, Julianna's grandmother had started working at the age of six, borne twelve children and nursed many more, and throughout remained an endless fount of love, joy, and strength. John, living in the City of Brotherly Love, saw homelessness and crime all around—and wondered if the aloha spirit would become a similarly hollow concept. "It made me realize that you must be intentional," he says, "and take risks to do what's right."

At the beginning of the millennium, the pair returned to Hawaiʻi. In 2000, John founded Pono Pacific, an enterprise in the fledgling industry of natural resource management; Julianna joined Pono Pacific in 2001. That year, Hawaiʻi's Department of Land and Natural Resources hired the company to revive the Youth Conservation Corps (YCC), a program designed to train young people in conservation by putting them to work in nature. John had been part of the YCC in the 1990s and had fallen in love with Hawaiʻi's ecosystems. Through Pono Pacific, the pair spent much of their time out in the field with young people: maintaining trails, planting native plants, restoring wetlands. It was not glamorous, but they loved it—and each other: They married in 2003.

opposite
John and Julianna with two of their keiki at Koa Ridge

In 2007, the Leongs founded the nonprofit Kupu as an offshoot of Pono Pacific, extending the reach of the YCC. Kupu now employs 400 young people every year, most of whom are paid; it places these interns with some eighty organizations, doing everything from energy audits to working on wind farms. Pono Pacific continues to expand, too; projects include restoring the Kalalau Trail and clearing Maunalua Bay of invasive algae.

Emma Yuen, an alumnus of the YCC program, spent a summer fresh out of Hilo High School alongside John and Julianna in 2002, controlling weeds, collecting seeds, clearing coastal areas, and eradicating coqui frogs. It was the best summer of her life, and it sparked a lifelong commitment to conservation work. She is full of praise for John and Julianna. "They took a risk and had a vision," she says. "They're increasing environmental awareness and affecting public policy." That vision keeps expanding: John and Julianna plan to take the Kupu model into the global community, especially into the islands of the Pacific. "Youth in the islands would love these opportunities," says Julianna. Adds John, who remains firmly committed to the power of intention: "It's about not drifting through life. We want to help build a sense of stewardship and leadership in other places."

CONTRIBUTORS

Catherine Mariko Black was born in Nairobi, Kenya, and moved to Hawai'i at age eight. After graduating from Punahou School in 1994, she received a BA in religious studies from Brown University. For the past fifteen years she has worked in journalism, community organizing, and strategic communications in San Francisco, Buenos Aires, and Hawai'i. She is currently the director of campaign communications at Punahou School.

Allegra Goodman, who graduated from Punahou in 1985, is the author of *Intuition, Paradise Park, Kaaterskill Falls, The Family Markowitz*, and *Total Immersion. The Other Side of the Island* is her first book for younger readers. Her fiction has appeared in the *New Yorker, Commentary, Ploughshares, Prize Stories: The O. Henry Awards*, and *Best American Short Stories.* Her essays and reviews have appeared in the *New York Times Book Review*, the *New Republic*, the *Boston Globe*, and the *American Scholar.* Raised in Honolulu, Goodman studied English and philosophy at Harvard University and received a PhD in English literature from Stanford University. She is the recipient of a Whiting Writers' Award, a Salon award for fiction, and a fellowship from the Radcliffe Institute for Advanced Study at Harvard University. She lives with her family in Cambridge, Massachusetts.

James Koshiba, a member of the Punahou Class of 1991, is the cofounder and former executive director of Kanu Hawaii, a nonprofit working to build a social movement for more sustainable, compassionate, and resilient communities rooted in island values and personal commitment to change. Since 2013, he has worked as a writer, community organizer, and consultant to nonprofit and educational organizations in Hawai'i and the western United States. Prior to founding Kanu Hawaii, Koshiba worked in community development finance as an investment analyst with Boston Community Capital and held adjunct faculty positions at the University of Hawai'i and Chaminade University of Honolulu, teaching courses in entrepreneurship and community economic development. He earned a BA from Brown University and an MA in Public Policy from the Harvard Kennedy School of Government. He was born and raised in Hawai'i, and now lives in Kaimukī.

Sara Lin, a 1999 Punahou graduate, is a freelance journalist and most recently was a founding editor of *Honolulu Civil Beat*, an online investigative news start-up launched by eBay founder and philanthropist Pierre Omidyar. A graduate of Princeton University, Lin is a former staff writer for the *Los Angeles Times* and the *Wall Street Journal.*

Davianna Pōmaika'i McGregor is a professor and founding member of the Department of Ethnic Studies at the University of Hawai'i at Mānoa, and a historian of Hawai'i and the Pacific Ocean. She is a member of Protect Kaho'olawe 'Ohana and sailed on the *Hōkūle'a* with Nainoa Thompson from Kanaloa Kaho'olawe to O'ahu.

Linny Morris, a member of the Punahou class of 1973, has been a professional photographer since graduating in 1978 from Parsons School of Design in Manhattan. She has completed assignments in Europe, Tahiti, Australia, and the United States, including on all of the main islands of Hawai'i. The book *Under the Hula Moon: Living in Hawai'i* featured her work (Crown Publishing, 1992). She has also created images for books about the Honolulu Academy of Arts, the Contemporary Museum, Queen Emma Summer Palace, and Hulihe'e Palace, as well as for *The Hawaiian House Now* (Abrams, 2007). In 2015, she was the photographer for *Merriman's Hawai'i* by Hawai'i restaurateur Peter Merriman.

Mindy Pennybacker, a 1970 Punahou graduate, has worked as a journalist in New York City and Honolulu, where she is currently a features staff writer at the *Honolulu Star-Advertiser*, and was former editor-in-chief of *Honolulu Weekly*. She graduated from Stanford University, where she was a Wallace Stegner Fellow, the University of Iowa Writers Workshop, and the King Hall School of Law at the University of California, Davis. The author of *Do One Green Thing: Saving the Earth through Simple, Everyday Choices*, she has been published in the *Atlantic Monthly*, *Fiction*, the *Nation*, the *New York Times*, *Martha Stewart's Whole Living*, and *The Green Guide*, where she was editor-in-chief and cofounder of thegreenguide.com.

Randall Roth is a University of Hawai'i law professor who has received the university's highest awards for classroom teaching and community service. He has served as the president of the Hawaii State Bar Association. In 2005 the City of Honolulu included him on its list of 100 individuals who have made lasting contributions to Honolulu over its 100-year history. He and Judge Samuel Pailthorpe King '33 wrote *Broken Trust*, which the Hawaii Book Publishers Association named "Book of the Year" in 2007.

Julia Flynn Siler is the author of *Lost Kingdom: Hawaii's Last Queen, the Sugar Kings, and America's First Imperial Adventure*. A graduate of Brown University and the Columbia University Graduate School of Journalism, Siler is a former staff writer and foreign correspondent for the *Wall Street Journal* and *Businessweek*. Her first book was the *New York Times* best seller, *The House of Mondavi*. A resident of Marin County, California, she is now at work on a history set in turn-of-the-century San Francisco.

George Staples is a botanist, formerly at the Bishop Museum and the Singapore Botanic Gardens, who has coauthored three books about plants and animals of Hawai'i: *Ethnic Culinary Herbs*, *Hawai'i's Invasive Species*, and the highly acclaimed reference manual *A Tropical Garden Flora*. He earned a PhD at Harvard University. His research currently focuses on the morning glory family and is leading to a monograph about these plants and their roles in cultures throughout the world.

Julia Steele, a writer, grew up living on islands in the Atlantic, the Mediterranean, and the Pacific. She is a graduate of Suva Grammar School, the University of Hawai'i at Mānoa, and Stanford Law School. She has a long-standing interest in island ecosystems.

Mary Vorsino is an award-winning Honolulu-based writer and communications specialist. Previously a full-time reporter for the *Honolulu Star-Advertiser*, her work has also appeared in the *New York Times* and *USA Today*. Vorsino holds an MA in education from Chaminade University of Honolulu and an MA in political science from the University of Hawai'i at Mānoa, where she is pursuing a PhD in education.

Yong Zhao is the presidential chair and the director of Global and Online Education at the University of Oregon. His research focuses on educational innovations in the age of globalization. His most recent book is *Who's Afraid of the Big Bad Dragon? Why China Has the Best (and Worst) Education System in the World*.

ILLUSTRATION CREDITS

Note: Feature photographs of the Punahou campus and portraits of James Scott, Constance Hee Lau, Susanna Moore, Kaui Hart Hemmings, and John and Julianna Rapu Leong were made by Linny Morris '73 in 2014 and 2015. Small graphic vignettes and illustrations that are scattered throughout the essays and profiles included in this book are from The Buff and Blue *and* Oahuan *yearbooks from 1900 to 1959 in the Punahou Archives collection; the program and souvenir booklet* The Seventy-Fifth Anniversary Pageant: Punahou, June 21, 1916 *in the Punahou Archives collection; and the book* Kimo: The Whistling Boy *by Alice Cooper (1907) Bailey, illustrated by Lucille Holling, in the Cooke Library collection. Shuzo Uemoto photographed for reproduction many of the illustrations from public and private collections noted within the illustration credits, including all of the nineteenth-century portraits.*

i: Hala. Photograph © Franco Salmoiraghi, 1978.

ii: Kapa moe, bark cloth, early nineteenth century. Mark and Carolyn Blackburn collection, Honolulu.

iii: Chiefs Boki and Liliha. Pencil, pastel, and gouache, by John Hayter, 1824. Sam and Mary Cooke collection.

iv–v: Grove of kukui trees, Kauaʻi. Engraving from an 1840 drawing by Alfred T. Agate, 1844. Sam and Mary Cooke collection.

vi: Night-blooming cereus at Punahou School. Photograph © Franco Salmoiraghi, 1991.

viii–ix: Alumni Lūʻau, 2014. Photograph by Linny Morris.

x: Oahu College class ring, 1838. Photograph by Linny Morris. Punahou Archives.

xiii: Julia Ann Eliza Gulick and Thomas L. Gulick. Ambrotype, 1860. Mission Houses Museum Library.

xiv: Letter from Abner Wilcox to W. D. Alexander, 1864. Mission Houses Museum Library.

xv: William H. Gulick, Nathaniel B. Emerson, Thomas L. Gulick, Samuel T. Alexander, and Albert B. Lyons. Ambrotype, 1859. Mission Houses Museum Library.

xvi–xvii: Mānoa Valley from Waikīkī. Oil painting by D. Howard Hitchcock, c. 1908. Sam and Mary Cooke collection.

xviii: Queen Kaʻahumanu. Lithograph with hand coloring from an 1817 watercolor sketch by Louis Choris, 1824. Sam and Mary Cooke collection.

2: Kauikeaouli (Kamehameha III). Daguerreotype, c. 1850. Bishop Museum.

3: Survey map of Kapunahou. Drawn by T. Metcalf, 1848. Hawaii State Archives.

4: John Papa ʻĪʻī. Daguerreotype, c. 1851. Bishop Museum.

5: Title page from *Ke Kaao o Laieikawai* by S. N. Haleʻole, 1863. Punahou Archives.

6: Levi Chamberlain. Daguerreotype, Boston, 1846. Mission Houses Museum Library.

6–7: Punahou School, 1846. Etching by H. N. Poole, 1916, from an 1846 drawing by Horton O. Knapp. Mission Houses Museum Library.

8–9: Old School Hall. Photograph by Linny Morris.

10: *Ka Palapala Hemolele a Iohova ko Kakou Akua*, 1838. Punahou Archives.

11: Night-blooming cereus. Photograph by Linny Morris.

12–13: Front gates of Punahou School. Photograph by Linny Morris.

13: Chief Abner Pākī. Daguerreotype, c. 1850. Bishop Museum.

14–15: Montague Hall. Photograph by Linny Morris.

16: Amos Starr Cooke and daughter Mary Annis. Daguerreotype by Hugo Stangenwald, 1853. Mission Houses Museum Library.

16: Juliet Montague Cooke and son Amos Francis. Daguerreotype by Hugo Stangenwald, 1853. Mission Houses Museum Library.

17: Montague Hall. Photograph by Linny Morris.

18: Bernice Pauahi Bishop and Charles Reed Bishop. Ambrotype, c. 1859. Bishop Museum.

19: Pauahi Hall. Photograph by Linny Morris.

20: Cooke Hall. Photograph by Linny Morris.

21: Emma Metcalf Beckley Nakuina. Carte de visite, n.d. Bishop Museum.

22: Kaakau. Ambrotype, c. 1865. Mission Houses Museum Library.

22: Willy Wilder. Ambrotype, c. 1865. Mission Houses Museum Library.

23: Poakahi. Ambrotype, c. 1860. Mission Houses Museum Library.

23: Maria Chamberlain. Ambrotype, c. 1860. Mission Houses Museum Library.

24: James Kapaeʻalii Scott. Photograph by Linny Morris.

26: Punahou campus at the Centennial. Painting by students of Helen Hitchcock Maxon, 1941. Punahou Archives.

30–31: President's Home. Photograph by Linny Morris.

36–37: Interior of President's Home. Photograph by Linny Morris.

37: Koa cabinet, President's Home. Photograph by Linny Morris.

42: Constance Hee Lau. Photograph by Linny Morris.

45: View from the President's Home. Photograph by Linny Morris.

46: Hōkūleʻa. Photograph © Monte Costa/Photo-ResourceHawaii.com, 1997.

48: Ceremony at Taputapuātea Marae, Raʻiātea. Photograph © Monte Costa/PhotoResourceHawaii. com, 1995.

50: Mamiya Science Center laboratory. Photograph by Linny Morris.

51: Mamiya Science Center mosaic. Photograph by Linny Morris.

52–53: The Academy Quadrangle. Photograph by Linny Morris.

54: Alexander Hall. Photograph by Linny Morris.

55: Rev. William P. Alexander. Daguerreotype by Hugo Stangenwald, c. 1855. Mission Houses Museum Library.

55: Arthur C. Alexander. Ambrotype, c. 1865. Mission Houses Museum Library.

56: Title page and frontispiece from *Memoirs of Henry Obookiah*, 1819. Punahou Archives.

56–57: Alexander Hall. Photograph by Linny Morris.

58–59: Stamping dies for medals and rings. Photograph by Linny Morris. Punahou Archives.

60–61: Alumni Lūʻau, 2014. Photograph by Linny Morris.

62: Plaque commemorating the gift of Kapunahou from Hawaiian chiefs, presented to the school in 1941. Photograph by Linny Morris.

63: Port of Honolulu. Lithograph with hand coloring from an 1816 drawing by Louis Choris, 1824. Sam and Mary Cooke collection.

64: Rev. Asa and Lucy Thurston. Ambrotype, c. 1864. Mission Houses Museum Library.

65: Rev. Lorenzo and Lucia Lyons. Daguerreotype by Hugo Stangenwald, 1856. Mission Houses Museum Library.

65: Rev. Peter and Fanny Gulick. Ambrotype, c. 1856. Mission Houses Museum Library.

66–67: Thurston Memorial Chapel. Photograph by Linny Morris.

68: Koa entrance, Thurston Memorial Chapel. Photograph by Linny Morris.

74–75: Thurston Memorial Chapel. Photograph by Linny Morris.

76–77: Interior, Thurston Memorial Chapel. Photograph by Linny Morris.

84: Rev. Dwight Baldwin. Daguerreotype by Hugo Stangenwald, Lahaina, c. 1853. Mission Houses Museum Library.

84: Charlotte Fowler Baldwin. Daguerreotype by Hugo Stangenwald, c. 1853. Mission Houses Museum Library.

85: Charles Fowler Baldwin. Daguerreotype by Hugo Stangenwald, c. 1853. Mission Houses Museum Library.

85: Julia Kealoha. Daguerreotype by Hugo Stangenwald, c. 1853. Mission Houses Museum Library.

86: Samuel P. King. Photograph, c. 1944. King family collection.

88: King family. Photograph, 1945. King family collection.

89: Judge Samuel P. King. Photograph © E. Y. Yanagi, 2004.

90: Paul Reppun and his granddaughter, Maka-kailenuiaola Diane Dickson, c. 1996. Photograph by Piliāmoʻo.

92: Reppun family. Photograph, c. 1978. Reppun family collection.

93–95: Third-Grade Lūʻau, 2014. Photographs by Linny Morris.

96–97: Castle Hall. Photograph by Linny Morris.

98: Case Middle School. Photograph by Linny Morris.

106–107: Bishop Hall. Photographs by Linny Morris.

108–109: Rice Field (Middle Field). Photograph by Linny Morris.

116: Beatrice Krauss. Detail of photograph, c. 1920. Krauss family collection.

116: Beatrice Krauss, c. 1987. Photographs by Franco Salmoiraghi.

118: Frontispiece and title page of *The Universal Conchologist*. Hand-colored engraving by Thomas Martyn, 1789. Sam and Mary Cooke collection.

119: E. Alison Kay, 1946. Punahou Archives.

121–123: Elizabeth P. Waterhouse Pool. Photographs by Linny Morris.

124: Susanna Moore. Photograph by Linny Morris.

126: Nora Okja Keller, 1996. Photograph by Marion Ettlinger.

127: Allegra Goodman, 1998. Photograph by Marion Ettlinger.

128: Kaui Hart Hemmings. Photograph by Linny Morris.

131: White bird of paradise. Photograph by Linny Morris.

132: Mrs. Mabel Hefty's fifth-grade class, 1972. Punahou Archives.

134–135: Castle Hall. Photograph by Linny Morris.

135: Barack Obama at Harvard Law School. Photograph © Joe Wrinn/Harvard University/Handout/Corbis, 1990.

138–139: Dillingham Hall and Old School Hall. Photograph by Linny Morris.

140: Dillingham Hall. Photograph by Linny Morris.

141: Map of the Punahou campus drawn by Baldwin and Alexander, 1917. Punahou Archives.

142–143: Dillingham Hall. Photograph by Linny Morris.

144–145: Variety Show, 2014, Dillingham Auditorium. Photographs by Linny Morris.

146–151: Punahou Carnival, 2014. Photographs by Linny Morris.

152–153: Punahou Carnival, from Rocky Hill, 2014. Photograph by Linny Morris.

152: Holokū pageant, 2014. Photograph by Linny Morris.

168: Vanessa Adams, Beko, Ethiopia. Photograph, c. 2014. Vanessa Adams collection.

171: Asa Thurston Physical Education Center. Photograph by Linny Morris.

172–173: Christopher B. Hemmeter Field House. Photograph by Linny Morris.

174–175: Alexander Field and Atherton Track. Photograph by Linny Morris.

174: Carissa Moore. Photograph by Michael Williams.

179: Football players, Alexander Field. Photograph by Linny Morris.

180: Omidyar K–1 Neighborhood. Photograph by Linny Morris.

184–185: Classroom, Omidyar K–1 Neighborhood. Photograph by Linny Morris.

188–189: Hawaiian Garden of the Overton Outdoor Learning Center. Photograph by Linny Morris.

192–193: Wilcox Hall. Photograph by Linny Morris.

195–197: Samuel and Mary Castle Art Center. Photographs by Linny Morris.

199: Case Middle School creative learning center. Photograph by Linny Morris.

204: Illustration by Lucille Hollings, from *Kimo: The Whistling Boy*, by Alice Cooper Bailey. New York: P. F. Volland Co., 1928, p. 76. Punahou Archives.

205: Byron Washom. Photograph, c. 1958. Byron Washom collection.

207: Wilcox Hall. Photograph by Linny Morris.

208: Steve Case. Photograph © Joanne S. Lawton/Washington Business Journal, Washington, DC, 2012.

208: Daniel H. and Carol Holmes Case. Photograph, 1954. Case family collection.

210: Case family. Photograph, c. 1973. Case family collection.

211–215: Baccalaureate, Central Union Church, 2014. Photographs by Linny Morris.

216: John and Julianna Rapu Leong and family. Photograph by Linny Morris.

218: Ivory pīkake lei. Photograph by Linny Morris. Punahou Archives.

INDEX